C-1341

CAREER EXAMINATION SERIES

THIS IS YOUR **PASSBOOK**® FOR ...

LAW ASSISTANT

NLC®

NATIONAL LEARNING CORPORATION®
passbooks.com

COPYRIGHT NOTICE

This book is SOLELY intended for, is sold ONLY to, and its use is RESTRICTED to individual, bona fide applicants or candidates who qualify by virtue of having seriously filed applications for appropriate license, certificate, professional and/or promotional advancement, higher school matriculation, scholarship, or other legitimate requirements of educational and/or governmental authorities.

This book is NOT intended for use, class instruction, tutoring, training, duplication, copying, reprinting, excerption, or adaptation, etc., by:

1) Other publishers
2) Proprietors and/or Instructors of «Coaching» and/or Preparatory Courses
3) Personnel and/or Training Divisions of commercial, industrial, and governmental organizations
4) Schools, colleges, or universities and/or their departments and staffs, including teachers and other personnel
5) Testing Agencies or Bureaus
6) Study groups which seek by the purchase of a single volume to copy and/or duplicate and/or adapt this material for use by the group as a whole without having purchased individual volumes for each of the members of the group
7) Et al.

Such persons would be in violation of appropriate Federal and State statutes.

PROVISION OF LICENSING AGREEMENTS. — Recognized educational, commercial, industrial, and governmental institutions and organizations, and others legitimately engaged in educational pursuits, including training, testing, and measurement activities, may address request for a licensing agreement to the copyright owners, who will determine whether, and under what conditions, including fees and charges, the materials in this book may be used them. In other words, a licensing facility exists for the legitimate use of the material in this book on other than an individual basis. However, it is asseverated and affirmed here that the material in this book CANNOT be used without the receipt of the express permission of such a licensing agreement from the Publishers. Inquiries re licensing should be addressed to the company, attention rights and permissions department.

All rights reserved, including the right of reproduction in whole or in part, in any form or by any means, electronic or mechanical, including photocopying, recording, or by any information storage and retrieval system, without permission in writing from the Publisher.

Copyright © 2020 by

NLC®

National Learning Corporation

212 Michael Drive, Syosset, NY 11791
(516) 921-8888 • www.passbooks.com
E-mail: info@passbooks.com

PUBLISHED IN THE UNITED STATES OF AMERICA

PASSBOOK® SERIES

THE *PASSBOOK® SERIES* has been created to prepare applicants and candidates for the ultimate academic battlefield – the examination room.

At some time in our lives, each and every one of us may be required to take an examination – for validation, matriculation, admission, qualification, registration, certification, or licensure.

Based on the assumption that every applicant or candidate has met the basic formal educational standards, has taken the required number of courses, and read the necessary texts, the *PASSBOOK® SERIES* furnishes the one special preparation which may assure passing with confidence, instead of failing with insecurity. Examination questions – together with answers – are furnished as the basic vehicle for study so that the mysteries of the examination and its compounding difficulties may be eliminated or diminished by a sure method.

This book is meant to help you pass your examination provided that you qualify and are serious in your objective.

The entire field is reviewed through the huge store of content information which is succinctly presented through a provocative and challenging approach – the question-and-answer method.

A climate of success is established by furnishing the correct answers at the end of each test.

You soon learn to recognize types of questions, forms of questions, and patterns of questioning. You may even begin to anticipate expected outcomes.

You perceive that many questions are repeated or adapted so that you can gain acute insights, which may enable you to score many sure points.

You learn how to confront new questions, or types of questions, and to attack them confidently and work out the correct answers.

You note objectives and emphases, and recognize pitfalls and dangers, so that you may make positive educational adjustments.

Moreover, you are kept fully informed in relation to new concepts, methods, practices, and directions in the field.

You discover that you arre actually taking the examination all the time: you are preparing for the examination by "taking" an examination, not by reading extraneous and/or supererogatory textbooks.

In short, this PASSBOOK®, used directedly, should be an important factor in helping you to pass your test.

LAW ASSISTANT

DUTIES
Assists in the review, research, and analysis of legal matters for a department or jurisdiction. Performs research and prepares opinions on points of law, interpretations, precedents, and other background material for administrative or court action. Prepares official, legal documents such as Petitions, Motions, and Orders. Participates in the negotiation and preparation of contracts with authorized individuals, or agencies. May assist in drafting departmental regulations and policy, and charter amendments or legislation, relevant to the department.

SCOPE OF THE WRITTEN TEST
The written test will be designed to cover knowledges, skills, and/or abilities in the following areas:
1. Understanding and interpreting written material;
2. Preparing written material; and
3. Legal research.

HOW TO TAKE A TEST

I. YOU MUST PASS AN EXAMINATION

A. *WHAT EVERY CANDIDATE SHOULD KNOW*

Examination applicants often ask us for help in preparing for the written test. What can I study in advance? What kinds of questions will be asked? How will the test be given? How will the papers be graded?

As an applicant for a civil service examination, you may be wondering about some of these things. Our purpose here is to suggest effective methods of advance study and to describe civil service examinations.

Your chances for success on this examination can be increased if you know how to prepare. Those "pre-examination jitters" can be reduced if you know what to expect. You can even experience an adventure in good citizenship if you know why civil service exams are given.

B. *WHY ARE CIVIL SERVICE EXAMINATIONS GIVEN?*

Civil service examinations are important to you in two ways. As a citizen, you want public jobs filled by employees who know how to do their work. As a job seeker, you want a fair chance to compete for that job on an equal footing with other candidates. The best-known means of accomplishing this two-fold goal is the competitive examination.

Exams are widely publicized throughout the nation. They may be administered for jobs in federal, state, city, municipal, town or village governments or agencies.

Any citizen may apply, with some limitations, such as the age or residence of applicants. Your experience and education may be reviewed to see whether you meet the requirements for the particular examination. When these requirements exist, they are reasonable and applied consistently to all applicants. Thus, a competitive examination may cause you some uneasiness now, but it is your privilege and safeguard.

C. *HOW ARE CIVIL SERVICE EXAMS DEVELOPED?*

Examinations are carefully written by trained technicians who are specialists in the field known as "psychological measurement," in consultation with recognized authorities in the field of work that the test will cover. These experts recommend the subject matter areas or skills to be tested; only those knowledges or skills important to your success on the job are included. The most reliable books and source materials available are used as references. Together, the experts and technicians judge the difficulty level of the questions.

Test technicians know how to phrase questions so that the problem is clearly stated. Their ethics do not permit "trick" or "catch" questions. Questions may have been tried out on sample groups, or subjected to statistical analysis, to determine their usefulness.

Written tests are often used in combination with performance tests, ratings of training and experience, and oral interviews. All of these measures combine to form the best-known means of finding the right person for the right job.

II. HOW TO PASS THE WRITTEN TEST

A. NATURE OF THE EXAMINATION

To prepare intelligently for civil service examinations, you should know how they differ from school examinations you have taken. In school you were assigned certain definite pages to read or subjects to cover. The examination questions were quite detailed and usually emphasized memory. Civil service exams, on the other hand, try to discover your present ability to perform the duties of a position, plus your potentiality to learn these duties. In other words, a civil service exam attempts to predict how successful you will be. Questions cover such a broad area that they cannot be as minute and detailed as school exam questions.

In the public service similar kinds of work, or positions, are grouped together in one "class." This process is known as *position-classification*. All the positions in a class are paid according to the salary range for that class. One class title covers all of these positions, and they are all tested by the same examination.

B. FOUR BASIC STEPS

1) Study the announcement

How, then, can you know what subjects to study? Our best answer is: "Learn as much as possible about the class of positions for which you've applied." The exam will test the knowledge, skills and abilities needed to do the work.

Your most valuable source of information about the position you want is the official exam announcement. This announcement lists the training and experience qualifications. Check these standards and apply only if you come reasonably close to meeting them.

The brief description of the position in the examination announcement offers some clues to the subjects which will be tested. Think about the job itself. Review the duties in your mind. Can you perform them, or are there some in which you are rusty? Fill in the blank spots in your preparation.

Many jurisdictions preview the written test in the exam announcement by including a section called "Knowledge and Abilities Required," "Scope of the Examination," or some similar heading. Here you will find out specifically what fields will be tested.

2) Review your own background

Once you learn in general what the position is all about, and what you need to know to do the work, ask yourself which subjects you already know fairly well and which need improvement. You may wonder whether to concentrate on improving your strong areas or on building some background in your fields of weakness. When the announcement has specified "some knowledge" or "considerable knowledge," or has used adjectives like "beginning principles of..." or "advanced ... methods," you can get a clue as to the number and difficulty of questions to be asked in any given field. More questions, and hence broader coverage, would be included for those subjects which are more important in the work. Now weigh your strengths and weaknesses against the job requirements and prepare accordingly.

3) Determine the level of the position

Another way to tell how intensively you should prepare is to understand the level of the job for which you are applying. Is it the entering level? In other words, is this the position in which beginners in a field of work are hired? Or is it an intermediate or advanced level? Sometimes this is indicated by such words as "Junior" or "Senior" in the class title. Other jurisdictions use Roman numerals to designate the level – Clerk I, Clerk II, for example. The word "Supervisor" sometimes appears in the title. If the level is not indicated by the title, check the description of duties. Will you be working under very close supervision, or will you have responsibility for independent decisions in this work?

4) Choose appropriate study materials

Now that you know the subjects to be examined and the relative amount of each subject to be covered, you can choose suitable study materials. For beginning level jobs, or even advanced ones, if you have a pronounced weakness in some aspect of your training, read a modern, standard textbook in that field. Be sure it is up to date and has general coverage. Such books are normally available at your library, and the librarian will be glad to help you locate one. For entry-level positions, questions of appropriate difficulty are chosen – neither highly advanced questions, nor those too simple. Such questions require careful thought but not advanced training.

If the position for which you are applying is technical or advanced, you will read more advanced, specialized material. If you are already familiar with the basic principles of your field, elementary textbooks would waste your time. Concentrate on advanced textbooks and technical periodicals. Think through the concepts and review difficult problems in your field.

These are all general sources. You can get more ideas on your own initiative, following these leads. For example, training manuals and publications of the government agency which employs workers in your field can be useful, particularly for technical and professional positions. A letter or visit to the government department involved may result in more specific study suggestions, and certainly will provide you with a more definite idea of the exact nature of the position you are seeking.

III. KINDS OF TESTS

Tests are used for purposes other than measuring knowledge and ability to perform specified duties. For some positions, it is equally important to test ability to make adjustments to new situations or to profit from training. In others, basic mental abilities not dependent on information are essential. Questions which test these things may not appear as pertinent to the duties of the position as those which test for knowledge and information. Yet they are often highly important parts of a fair examination. For very general questions, it is almost impossible to help you direct your study efforts. What we can do is to point out some of the more common of these general abilities needed in public service positions and describe some typical questions.

1) General information

Broad, general information has been found useful for predicting job success in some kinds of work. This is tested in a variety of ways, from vocabulary lists to questions about current events. Basic background in some field of work, such as sociology or economics, may be sampled in a group of questions. Often these are principles which have become familiar to most persons through exposure rather than through formal training. It is difficult to advise you how to study for these questions; being alert to the world around you is our best suggestion.

2) Verbal ability

An example of an ability needed in many positions is verbal or language ability. Verbal ability is, in brief, the ability to use and understand words. Vocabulary and grammar tests are typical measures of this ability. Reading comprehension or paragraph interpretation questions are common in many kinds of civil service tests. You are given a paragraph of written material and asked to find its central meaning.

3) Numerical ability

Number skills can be tested by the familiar arithmetic problem, by checking paired lists of numbers to see which are alike and which are different, or by interpreting charts and graphs. In the latter test, a graph may be printed in the test booklet which you are asked to use as the basis for answering questions.

4) Observation

A popular test for law-enforcement positions is the observation test. A picture is shown to you for several minutes, then taken away. Questions about the picture test your ability to observe both details and larger elements.

5) Following directions

In many positions in the public service, the employee must be able to carry out written instructions dependably and accurately. You may be given a chart with several columns, each column listing a variety of information. The questions require you to carry out directions involving the information given in the chart.

6) Skills and aptitudes

Performance tests effectively measure some manual skills and aptitudes. When the skill is one in which you are trained, such as typing or shorthand, you can practice. These tests are often very much like those given in business school or high school courses. For many of the other skills and aptitudes, however, no short-time preparation can be made. Skills and abilities natural to you or that you have developed throughout your lifetime are being tested.

Many of the general questions just described provide all the data needed to answer the questions and ask you to use your reasoning ability to find the answers. Your best preparation for these tests, as well as for tests of facts and ideas, is to be at your physical and mental best. You, no doubt, have your own methods of getting into an exam-taking mood and keeping "in shape." The next section lists some ideas on this subject.

IV. KINDS OF QUESTIONS

Only rarely is the "essay" question, which you answer in narrative form, used in civil service tests. Civil service tests are usually of the short-answer type. Full instructions for answering these questions will be given to you at the examination. But in case this is your first experience with short-answer questions and separate answer sheets, here is what you need to know:

1) Multiple-choice Questions

Most popular of the short-answer questions is the "multiple choice" or "best answer" question. It can be used, for example, to test for factual knowledge, ability to solve problems or judgment in meeting situations found at work.

A multiple-choice question is normally one of three types—

- It can begin with an incomplete statement followed by several possible endings. You are to find the one ending which *best* completes the statement, although some of the others may not be entirely wrong.
- It can also be a complete statement in the form of a question which is answered by choosing one of the statements listed.
- It can be in the form of a problem – again you select the best answer.

Here is an example of a multiple-choice question with a discussion which should give you some clues as to the method for choosing the right answer:

When an employee has a complaint about his assignment, the action which will *best* help him overcome his difficulty is to
- A. discuss his difficulty with his coworkers
- B. take the problem to the head of the organization
- C. take the problem to the person who gave him the assignment
- D. say nothing to anyone about his complaint

In answering this question, you should study each of the choices to find which is best. Consider choice "A" – Certainly an employee may discuss his complaint with fellow employees, but no change or improvement can result, and the complaint remains unresolved. Choice "B" is a poor choice since the head of the organization probably does not know what assignment you have been given, and taking your problem to him is known as "going over the head" of the supervisor. The supervisor, or person who made the assignment, is the person who can clarify it or correct any injustice. Choice "C" is, therefore, correct. To say nothing, as in choice "D," is unwise. Supervisors have and interest in knowing the problems employees are facing, and the employee is seeking a solution to his problem.

2) True/False Questions

The "true/false" or "right/wrong" form of question is sometimes used. Here a complete statement is given. Your job is to decide whether the statement is right or wrong.

SAMPLE: A roaming cell-phone call to a nearby city costs less than a non-roaming call to a distant city.

This statement is wrong, or false, since roaming calls are more expensive.

This is not a complete list of all possible question forms, although most of the others are variations of these common types. You will always get complete directions for answering questions. Be sure you understand *how* to mark your answers – ask questions until you do.

V. RECORDING YOUR ANSWERS

Computer terminals are used more and more today for many different kinds of exams.

For an examination with very few applicants, you may be told to record your answers in the test booklet itself. Separate answer sheets are much more common. If this separate answer sheet is to be scored by machine – and this is often the case – it is highly important that you mark your answers correctly in order to get credit.

An electronic scoring machine is often used in civil service offices because of the speed with which papers can be scored. Machine-scored answer sheets must be marked with a pencil, which will be given to you. This pencil has a high graphite content which responds to the electronic scoring machine. As a matter of fact, stray dots may register as answers, so do not let your pencil rest on the answer sheet while you are pondering the correct answer. Also, if your pencil lead breaks or is otherwise defective, ask for another.

Since the answer sheet will be dropped in a slot in the scoring machine, be careful not to bend the corners or get the paper crumpled.

The answer sheet normally has five vertical columns of numbers, with 30 numbers to a column. These numbers correspond to the question numbers in your test booklet. After each number, going across the page are four or five pairs of dotted lines. These short dotted lines have small letters or numbers above them. The first two pairs may also have a "T" or "F" above the letters. This indicates that the first two pairs only are to be used if the questions are of the true-false type. If the questions are multiple choice, disregard the "T" and "F" and pay attention only to the small letters or numbers.

Answer your questions in the manner of the sample that follows:

32. The largest city in the United States is
    A. Washington, D.C.
    B. New York City
    C. Chicago
    D. Detroit
    E. San Francisco

1) Choose the answer you think is best. (New York City is the largest, so "B" is correct.)
2) Find the row of dotted lines numbered the same as the question you are answering. (Find row number 32)
3) Find the pair of dotted lines corresponding to the answer. (Find the pair of lines under the mark "B.")
4) Make a solid black mark between the dotted lines.

VI. BEFORE THE TEST

Common sense will help you find procedures to follow to get ready for an examination. Too many of us, however, overlook these sensible measures. Indeed, nervousness and fatigue have been found to be the most serious reasons why applicants fail to do their best on civil service tests. Here is a list of reminders:

- Begin your preparation early – Don't wait until the last minute to go scurrying around for books and materials or to find out what the position is all about.
- Prepare continuously – An hour a night for a week is better than an all-night cram session. This has been definitely established. What is more, a night a week for a month will return better dividends than crowding your study into a shorter period of time.
- Locate the place of the exam – You have been sent a notice telling you when and where to report for the examination. If the location is in a different town or otherwise unfamiliar to you, it would be well to inquire the best route and learn something about the building.
- Relax the night before the test – Allow your mind to rest. Do not study at all that night. Plan some mild recreation or diversion; then go to bed early and get a good night's sleep.
- Get up early enough to make a leisurely trip to the place for the test – This way unforeseen events, traffic snarls, unfamiliar buildings, etc. will not upset you.
- Dress comfortably – A written test is not a fashion show. You will be known by number and not by name, so wear something comfortable.
- Leave excess paraphernalia at home – Shopping bags and odd bundles will get in your way. You need bring only the items mentioned in the official notice you received; usually everything you need is provided. Do not bring reference books to the exam. They will only confuse those last minutes and be taken away from you when in the test room.
- Arrive somewhat ahead of time – If because of transportation schedules you must get there very early, bring a newspaper or magazine to take your mind off yourself while waiting.
- Locate the examination room – When you have found the proper room, you will be directed to the seat or part of the room where you will sit. Sometimes you are given a sheet of instructions to read while you are waiting. Do not fill out any forms until you are told to do so; just read them and be prepared.
- Relax and prepare to listen to the instructions
- If you have any physical problem that may keep you from doing your best, be sure to tell the test administrator. If you are sick or in poor health, you really cannot do your best on the exam. You can come back and take the test some other time.

VII. AT THE TEST

The day of the test is here and you have the test booklet in your hand. The temptation to get going is very strong. Caution! There is more to success than knowing the right answers. You must know how to identify your papers and understand variations in the type of short-answer question used in this particular examination. Follow these suggestions for maximum results from your efforts:

1) Cooperate with the monitor
  The test administrator has a duty to create a situation in which you can be as much at ease as possible. He will give instructions, tell you when to begin, check to see that you are marking your answer sheet correctly, and so on. He is not there to guard you, although he will see that your competitors do not take unfair advantage. He wants to help you do your best.

2) Listen to all instructions
  Don't jump the gun! Wait until you understand all directions. In most civil service tests you get more time than you need to answer the questions. So don't be in a hurry. Read each word of instructions until you clearly understand the meaning. Study the examples, listen to all announcements and follow directions. Ask questions if you do not understand what to do.

3) Identify your papers
  Civil service exams are usually identified by number only. You will be assigned a number; you must not put your name on your test papers. Be sure to copy your number correctly. Since more than one exam may be given, copy your exact examination title.

4) Plan your time
  Unless you are told that a test is a "speed" or "rate of work" test, speed itself is usually not important. Time enough to answer all the questions will be provided, but this does not mean that you have all day. An overall time limit has been set. Divide the total time (in minutes) by the number of questions to determine the approximate time you have for each question.

5) Do not linger over difficult questions
  If you come across a difficult question, mark it with a paper clip (useful to have along) and come back to it when you have been through the booklet. One caution if you do this – be sure to skip a number on your answer sheet as well. Check often to be sure that you have not lost your place and that you are marking in the row numbered the same as the question you are answering.

6) Read the questions
  Be sure you know what the question asks! Many capable people are unsuccessful because they failed to *read* the questions correctly.

7) Answer all questions
  Unless you have been instructed that a penalty will be deducted for incorrect answers, it is better to guess than to omit a question.

8) Speed tests
  It is often better NOT to guess on speed tests. It has been found that on timed tests people are tempted to spend the last few seconds before time is called in marking answers at random – without even reading them – in the hope of picking up a few extra points. To discourage this practice, the instructions may warn you that your score will be "corrected" for guessing. That is, a penalty will be applied. The incorrect answers will be deducted from the correct ones, or some other penalty formula will be used.

9) Review your answers

If you finish before time is called, go back to the questions you guessed or omitted to give them further thought. Review other answers if you have time.

10) Return your test materials

If you are ready to leave before others have finished or time is called, take ALL your materials to the monitor and leave quietly. Never take any test material with you. The monitor can discover whose papers are not complete, and taking a test booklet may be grounds for disqualification.

VIII. EXAMINATION TECHNIQUES

1) Read the general instructions carefully. These are usually printed on the first page of the exam booklet. As a rule, these instructions refer to the timing of the examination; the fact that you should not start work until the signal and must stop work at a signal, etc. If there are any *special* instructions, such as a choice of questions to be answered, make sure that you note this instruction carefully.

2) When you are ready to start work on the examination, that is as soon as the signal has been given, read the instructions to each question booklet, underline any key words or phrases, such as *least, best, outline, describe* and the like. In this way you will tend to answer as requested rather than discover on reviewing your paper that you *listed without describing*, that you selected the *worst* choice rather than the *best* choice, etc.

3) If the examination is of the objective or multiple-choice type – that is, each question will also give a series of possible answers: A, B, C or D, and you are called upon to select the best answer and write the letter next to that answer on your answer paper – it is advisable to start answering each question in turn. There may be anywhere from 50 to 100 such questions in the three or four hours allotted and you can see how much time would be taken if you read through all the questions before beginning to answer any. Furthermore, if you come across a question or group of questions which you know would be difficult to answer, it would undoubtedly affect your handling of all the other questions.

4) If the examination is of the essay type and contains but a few questions, it is a moot point as to whether you should read all the questions before starting to answer any one. Of course, if you are given a choice – say five out of seven and the like – then it is essential to read all the questions so you can eliminate the two that are most difficult. If, however, you are asked to answer all the questions, there may be danger in trying to answer the easiest one first because you may find that you will spend too much time on it. The best technique is to answer the first question, then proceed to the second, etc.

5) Time your answers. Before the exam begins, write down the time it started, then add the time allowed for the examination and write down the time it must be completed, then divide the time available somewhat as follows:

- If 3-1/2 hours are allowed, that would be 210 minutes. If you have 80 objective-type questions, that would be an average of 2-1/2 minutes per question. Allow yourself no more than 2 minutes per question, or a total of 160 minutes, which will permit about 50 minutes to review.
- If for the time allotment of 210 minutes there are 7 essay questions to answer, that would average about 30 minutes a question. Give yourself only 25 minutes per question so that you have about 35 minutes to review.

6) The most important instruction is to *read each question* and make sure you know what is wanted. The second most important instruction is to *time yourself properly* so that you answer every question. The third most important instruction is to *answer every question*. Guess if you have to but include something for each question. Remember that you will receive no credit for a blank and will probably receive some credit if you write something in answer to an essay question. If you guess a letter – say "B" for a multiple-choice question – you may have guessed right. If you leave a blank as an answer to a multiple-choice question, the examiners may respect your feelings but it will not add a point to your score. Some exams may penalize you for wrong answers, so in such cases *only*, you may not want to guess unless you have some basis for your answer.

7) Suggestions
   a. Objective-type questions
      1. Examine the question booklet for proper sequence of pages and questions
      2. Read all instructions carefully
      3. Skip any question which seems too difficult; return to it after all other questions have been answered
      4. Apportion your time properly; do not spend too much time on any single question or group of questions
      5. Note and underline key words – *all, most, fewest, least, best, worst, same, opposite,* etc.
      6. Pay particular attention to negatives
      7. Note unusual option, e.g., unduly long, short, complex, different or similar in content to the body of the question
      8. Observe the use of "hedging" words – *probably, may, most likely,* etc.
      9. Make sure that your answer is put next to the same number as the question
      10. Do not second-guess unless you have good reason to believe the second answer is definitely more correct
      11. Cross out original answer if you decide another answer is more accurate; do not erase until you are ready to hand your paper in
      12. Answer all questions; guess unless instructed otherwise
      13. Leave time for review

   b. Essay questions
      1. Read each question carefully
      2. Determine exactly what is wanted. Underline key words or phrases.
      3. Decide on outline or paragraph answer

4. Include many different points and elements unless asked to develop any one or two points or elements
5. Show impartiality by giving pros and cons unless directed to select one side only
6. Make and write down any assumptions you find necessary to answer the questions
7. Watch your English, grammar, punctuation and choice of words
8. Time your answers; don't crowd material

8) Answering the essay question

Most essay questions can be answered by framing the specific response around several key words or ideas. Here are a few such key words or ideas:

M's: manpower, materials, methods, money, management
P's: purpose, program, policy, plan, procedure, practice, problems, pitfalls, personnel, public relations

   a. Six basic steps in handling problems:
      1. Preliminary plan and background development
      2. Collect information, data and facts
      3. Analyze and interpret information, data and facts
      4. Analyze and develop solutions as well as make recommendations
      5. Prepare report and sell recommendations
      6. Install recommendations and follow up effectiveness

   b. Pitfalls to avoid
      1. *Taking things for granted* – A statement of the situation does not necessarily imply that each of the elements is necessarily true; for example, a complaint may be invalid and biased so that all that can be taken for granted is that a complaint has been registered
      2. *Considering only one side of a situation* – Wherever possible, indicate several alternatives and then point out the reasons you selected the best one
      3. *Failing to indicate follow up* – Whenever your answer indicates action on your part, make certain that you will take proper follow-up action to see how successful your recommendations, procedures or actions turn out to be
      4. *Taking too long in answering any single question* – Remember to time your answers properly

IX. AFTER THE TEST

Scoring procedures differ in detail among civil service jurisdictions although the general principles are the same. Whether the papers are hand-scored or graded by machine we have described, they are nearly always graded by number. That is, the person who marks the paper knows only the number – never the name – of the applicant. Not until all the papers have been graded will they be matched with names. If other tests, such as training and experience or oral interview ratings have been given, scores will be combined. Different parts of the examination usually have different weights. For example, the written test might count 60 percent of the final grade, and a rating of training and experience 40 percent. In many jurisdictions, veterans will have a certain number of points added to their grades.

After the final grade has been determined, the names are placed in grade order and an eligible list is established. There are various methods for resolving ties between those who get the same final grade – probably the most common is to place first the name of the person whose application was received first. Job offers are made from the eligible list in the order the names appear on it. You will be notified of your grade and your rank as soon as all these computations have been made. This will be done as rapidly as possible.

People who are found to meet the requirements in the announcement are called "eligibles." Their names are put on a list of eligible candidates. An eligible's chances of getting a job depend on how high he stands on this list and how fast agencies are filling jobs from the list.

When a job is to be filled from a list of eligibles, the agency asks for the names of people on the list of eligibles for that job. When the civil service commission receives this request, it sends to the agency the names of the three people highest on this list. Or, if the job to be filled has specialized requirements, the office sends the agency the names of the top three persons who meet these requirements from the general list.

The appointing officer makes a choice from among the three people whose names were sent to him. If the selected person accepts the appointment, the names of the others are put back on the list to be considered for future openings.

That is the rule in hiring from all kinds of eligible lists, whether they are for typist, carpenter, chemist, or something else. For every vacancy, the appointing officer has his choice of any one of the top three eligibles on the list. This explains why the person whose name is on top of the list sometimes does not get an appointment when some of the persons lower on the list do. If the appointing officer chooses the second or third eligible, the No. 1 eligible does not get a job at once, but stays on the list until he is appointed or the list is terminated.

X. HOW TO PASS THE INTERVIEW TEST

The examination for which you applied requires an oral interview test. You have already taken the written test and you are now being called for the interview test – the final part of the formal examination.

You may think that it is not possible to prepare for an interview test and that there are no procedures to follow during an interview. Our purpose is to point out some things you can do in advance that will help you and some good rules to follow and pitfalls to avoid while you are being interviewed.

What is an interview supposed to test?

The written examination is designed to test the technical knowledge and competence of the candidate; the oral is designed to evaluate intangible qualities, not readily measured otherwise, and to establish a list showing the relative fitness of each candidate – as measured against his competitors – for the position sought. Scoring is not on the basis of "right" and "wrong," but on a sliding scale of values ranging from "not passable" to "outstanding." As a matter of fact, it is possible to achieve a relatively low score without a single "incorrect" answer because of evident weakness in the qualities being measured.

Occasionally, an examination may consist entirely of an oral test – either an individual or a group oral. In such cases, information is sought concerning the technical knowledges and abilities of the candidate, since there has been no written examination for this purpose. More commonly, however, an oral test is used to supplement a written examination.

Who conducts interviews?

The composition of oral boards varies among different jurisdictions. In nearly all, a representative of the personnel department serves as chairman. One of the members of the board may be a representative of the department in which the candidate would work. In some cases, "outside experts" are used, and, frequently, a businessman or some other representative of the general public is asked to serve. Labor and management or other special groups may be represented. The aim is to secure the services of experts in the appropriate field.

However the board is composed, it is a good idea (and not at all improper or unethical) to ascertain in advance of the interview who the members are and what groups they represent. When you are introduced to them, you will have some idea of their backgrounds and interests, and at least you will not stutter and stammer over their names.

What should be done before the interview?

While knowledge about the board members is useful and takes some of the surprise element out of the interview, there is other preparation which is more substantive. It *is* possible to prepare for an oral interview – in several ways:

1) Keep a copy of your application and review it carefully before the interview

This may be the only document before the oral board, and the starting point of the interview. Know what education and experience you have listed there, and the sequence and dates of all of it. Sometimes the board will ask you to review the highlights of your experience for them; you should not have to hem and haw doing it.

2) Study the class specification and the examination announcement

Usually, the oral board has one or both of these to guide them. The qualities, characteristics or knowledges required by the position sought are stated in these documents. They offer valuable clues as to the nature of the oral interview. For example, if the job involves supervisory responsibilities, the announcement will usually indicate that knowledge of modern supervisory methods and the qualifications of the candidate as a supervisor will be tested. If so, you can expect such questions, frequently in the form of a hypothetical situation which you are expected to solve. NEVER go into an oral without knowledge of the duties and responsibilities of the job you seek.

3) Think through each qualification required

Try to visualize the kind of questions you would ask if you were a board member. How well could you answer them? Try especially to appraise your own knowledge and background in each area, *measured against the job sought*, and identify any areas in which you are weak. Be critical and realistic – do not flatter yourself.

4) Do some general reading in areas in which you feel you may be weak

For example, if the job involves supervision and your past experience has NOT, some general reading in supervisory methods and practices, particularly in the field of human relations, might be useful. Do NOT study agency procedures or detailed manuals. The oral board will be testing your understanding and capacity, not your memory.

5) Get a good night's sleep and watch your general health and mental attitude

You will want a clear head at the interview. Take care of a cold or any other minor ailment, and of course, no hangovers.

What should be done on the day of the interview?

Now comes the day of the interview itself. Give yourself plenty of time to get there. Plan to arrive somewhat ahead of the scheduled time, particularly if your appointment is in the fore part of the day. If a previous candidate fails to appear, the board might be ready for you a bit early. By early afternoon an oral board is almost invariably behind schedule if there are many candidates, and you may have to wait. Take along a book or magazine to read, or your application to review, but leave any extraneous material in the waiting room when you go in for your interview. In any event, relax and compose yourself.

The matter of dress is important. The board is forming impressions about you – from your experience, your manners, your attitude, and your appearance. Give your personal appearance careful attention. Dress your best, but not your flashiest. Choose conservative, appropriate clothing, and be sure it is immaculate. This is a business interview, and your appearance should indicate that you regard it as such. Besides, being well groomed and properly dressed will help boost your confidence.

Sooner or later, someone will call your name and escort you into the interview room. *This is it.* From here on you are on your own. It is too late for any more preparation. But remember, you asked for this opportunity to prove your fitness, and you are here because your request was granted.

What happens when you go in?

The usual sequence of events will be as follows: The clerk (who is often the board stenographer) will introduce you to the chairman of the oral board, who will introduce you to the other members of the board. Acknowledge the introductions before you sit down. Do not be surprised if you find a microphone facing you or a stenotypist sitting by. Oral interviews are usually recorded in the event of an appeal or other review.

Usually the chairman of the board will open the interview by reviewing the highlights of your education and work experience from your application – primarily for the benefit of the other members of the board, as well as to get the material into the record. Do not interrupt or comment unless there is an error or significant misinterpretation; if that is the case, do not hesitate. But do not quibble about insignificant matters. Also, he will usually ask you some question about your education, experience or your present job – partly to get you to start talking and to establish the interviewing "rapport." He may start the actual questioning, or turn it over to one of the other members. Frequently, each member undertakes the questioning on a particular area, one in which he is perhaps most competent, so you can expect each member to participate in the examination. Because time is limited, you may also expect some rather abrupt switches in the direction the questioning takes, so do not be upset by it. Normally, a board member will not pursue a single line of questioning unless he discovers a particular strength or weakness.

After each member has participated, the chairman will usually ask whether any member has any further questions, then will ask you if you have anything you wish to add. Unless you are expecting this question, it may floor you. Worse, it may start you off on an extended, extemporaneous speech. The board is not usually seeking more information. The question is principally to offer you a last opportunity to present further qualifications or to indicate that you have nothing to add. So, if you feel that a significant qualification or characteristic has been overlooked, it is proper to point it out in a sentence or so. Do not compliment the board on the thoroughness of their examination – they have been sketchy, and you know it. If you wish, merely say, "No thank you, I have nothing further to add." This is a point where you can "talk yourself out" of a good impression or fail to present an important bit of information. Remember, *you close the interview yourself.*

The chairman will then say, "That is all, Mr. _____, thank you." Do not be startled; the interview is over, and quicker than you think. Thank him, gather your belongings and take your leave. Save your sigh of relief for the other side of the door.

How to put your best foot forward

Throughout this entire process, you may feel that the board individually and collectively is trying to pierce your defenses, seek out your hidden weaknesses and embarrass and confuse you. Actually, this is not true. They are obliged to make an appraisal of your qualifications for the job you are seeking, and they want to see you in your best light. Remember, they must interview all candidates and a non-cooperative candidate may become a failure in spite of their best efforts to bring out his qualifications. Here are 15 suggestions that will help you:

1) Be natural – Keep your attitude confident, not cocky

If you are not confident that you can do the job, do not expect the board to be. Do not apologize for your weaknesses, try to bring out your strong points. The board is interested in a positive, not negative, presentation. Cockiness will antagonize any board member and make him wonder if you are covering up a weakness by a false show of strength.

2) Get comfortable, but don't lounge or sprawl

Sit erectly but not stiffly. A careless posture may lead the board to conclude that you are careless in other things, or at least that you are not impressed by the importance of the occasion. Either conclusion is natural, even if incorrect. Do not fuss with your clothing, a pencil or an ashtray. Your hands may occasionally be useful to emphasize a point; do not let them become a point of distraction.

3) Do not wisecrack or make small talk

This is a serious situation, and your attitude should show that you consider it as such. Further, the time of the board is limited – they do not want to waste it, and neither should you.

4) Do not exaggerate your experience or abilities

In the first place, from information in the application or other interviews and sources, the board may know more about you than you think. Secondly, you probably will not get away with it. An experienced board is rather adept at spotting such a situation, so do not take the chance.

5) If you know a board member, do not make a point of it, yet do not hide it

Certainly you are not fooling him, and probably not the other members of the board. Do not try to take advantage of your acquaintanceship – it will probably do you little good.

6) Do not dominate the interview

Let the board do that. They will give you the clues – do not assume that you have to do all the talking. Realize that the board has a number of questions to ask you, and do not try to take up all the interview time by showing off your extensive knowledge of the answer to the first one.

7) Be attentive

You only have 20 minutes or so, and you should keep your attention at its sharpest throughout. When a member is addressing a problem or question to you, give him your undivided attention. Address your reply principally to him, but do not exclude the other board members.

8) Do not interrupt

A board member may be stating a problem for you to analyze. He will ask you a question when the time comes. Let him state the problem, and wait for the question.

9) Make sure you understand the question

Do not try to answer until you are sure what the question is. If it is not clear, restate it in your own words or ask the board member to clarify it for you. However, do not haggle about minor elements.

10) Reply promptly but not hastily

A common entry on oral board rating sheets is "candidate responded readily," or "candidate hesitated in replies." Respond as promptly and quickly as you can, but do not jump to a hasty, ill-considered answer.

11) Do not be peremptory in your answers

A brief answer is proper – but do not fire your answer back. That is a losing game from your point of view. The board member can probably ask questions much faster than you can answer them.

12) Do not try to create the answer you think the board member wants

He is interested in what kind of mind you have and how it works – not in playing games. Furthermore, he can usually spot this practice and will actually grade you down on it.

13) Do not switch sides in your reply merely to agree with a board member

Frequently, a member will take a contrary position merely to draw you out and to see if you are willing and able to defend your point of view. Do not start a debate, yet do not surrender a good position. If a position is worth taking, it is worth defending.

14) Do not be afraid to admit an error in judgment if you are shown to be wrong

The board knows that you are forced to reply without any opportunity for careful consideration. Your answer may be demonstrably wrong. If so, admit it and get on with the interview.

15) Do not dwell at length on your present job

The opening question may relate to your present assignment. Answer the question but do not go into an extended discussion. You are being examined for a *new* job, not your present one. As a matter of fact, try to phrase ALL your answers in terms of the job for which you are being examined.

Basis of Rating

Probably you will forget most of these "do's" and "don'ts" when you walk into the oral interview room. Even remembering them all will not ensure you a passing grade. Perhaps you did not have the qualifications in the first place. But remembering them will help you to put your best foot forward, without treading on the toes of the board members.

Rumor and popular opinion to the contrary notwithstanding, an oral board wants you to make the best appearance possible. They know you are under pressure – but they also want to see how you respond to it as a guide to what your reaction would be under the pressures of the job you seek. They will be influenced by the degree of poise you display, the personal traits you show and the manner in which you respond.

ABOUT THIS BOOK

This book contains tests divided into Examination Sections. Go through each test, answering every question in the margin. At the end of each test look at the answer key and check your answers. On the ones you got wrong, look at the right answer choice and learn. Do not fill in the answers first. Do not memorize the questions and answers, but understand the answer and principles involved. On your test, the questions will likely be different from the samples. Questions are changed and new ones added. If you understand these past questions you should have success with any changes that arise. Tests may consist of several types of questions. We have additional books on each subject should more study be advisable or necessary for you. Finally, the more you study, the better prepared you will be. This book is intended to be the last thing you study before you walk into the examination room. Prior study of relevant texts is also recommended. NLC publishes some of these in our Fundamental Series. Knowledge and good sense are important factors in passing your exam. Good luck also helps. So now study this Passbook, absorb the material contained within and take that knowledge into the examination. Then do your best to pass that exam.

EXAMINATION SECTION

EXAMINATION SECTION
TEST 1

DIRECTIONS: Each question or incomplete statement is followed by several suggested answers or completions. Select the one that BEST answers the question or completes the statement. *PRINT THE LETTER OF THE CORRECT ANSWER IN THE SPACE AT THE RIGHT.*

Questions 1-4.

DIRECTIONS: Questions 1 through 4 are to be answered on the basis of the following passage.

Those engaged in the exercise of First Amendment rights by pickets, marches, parades, and open-air assemblies are not exempted from obeying valid local traffic ordinances. In a recent pronouncement, Mr. Justice Baxter, speaking for the Supreme Court, wrote:

The rights of free speech and assembly, while fundamental to our democratic society, still do not mean that everyone with opinions or beliefs to express may address a group at any public place and at any time. The constitutional guarantee of liberty implies the existence of an organized society maintaining public order, without which liberty itself would be lost in the excesses of anarchy. The control of travel on the streets is a clear example of governmental responsibility to insure this necessary order. A restriction in that relation, designed to promote the public convenience in the interest of all, and not susceptible to abuses of discriminatory application, cannot be disregarded by the attempted exercise of some civil rights which, in other circumstances, would be entitled to protection. One would not be justified in ignoring the familiar red light because this was thought to be a means of social protest. Governmental authorities have the duty and responsibility to keep their streets open and available for movement. A group of demonstrators could not insist upon the right to cordon off a street, or entrance to a public or private building, and allow no one to pass who did not agree to listen to their exhortations.

1. Which of the following statements BEST reflects Mr. Justice Baxter's view of the relationship between liberty and public order?

    A. Public order cannot exist without liberty.
    B. Liberty cannot exist without public order.
    C. The existence of liberty undermines the existence of public order.
    D. The maintenance of public order insures the existence of liberty.

1.____

2. According to the above passage, local traffic ordinances result from

    A. governmental limitations on individual liberty
    B. governmental responsibility to insure public order
    C. majority rule as determined by democratic procedures
    D. restrictions on expression of dissent

2.____

3. The foregoing passage suggests that government would be acting IMPROPERLY if a local traffic ordinance

    A. was enforced in a discriminatory manner
    B. resulted in public inconvenience

3.____

C. violated the right of free speech and assembly
D. was not essential to public order

4. Of the following, the MOST appropriate title for the above passage is:

   A. THE RIGHTS OF FREE SPEECH AND ASSEMBLY
   B. ENFORCEMENT OF LOCAL TRAFFIC ORDINANCES
   C. FIRST AMENDMENT RIGHTS AND LOCAL TRAFFIC ORDINANCES
   D. LIBERTY AND ANARCHY

Questions 5-8.

DIRECTIONS: Questions 5 through 8 are to be answered on the basis of the following passage.

On November 8, 1976, the Supreme Court refused to block the payment of Medicaid funds for elective abortions. The Court's action means that a new Federal statute that bars the use of Federal funds for abortions unless abortion is necessary to save the life of the mother will not go into effect for many months, if at all.

A Federal District Court in Brooklyn ruled the following month that the statute was unconstitutional and ordered that Federal reimbursement for the costs of abortions continue on the same basis as reimbursements for the costs of pregnancy and childbirth-related services.

Technically, what the Court did today was to deny a request by Senator Howard Ramsdell and others for a stay blocking enforcement of the District Court order pending appeal. The Court's action was a victory for New York City. The City's Health and Hospitals Corporation initiated one of the two lawsuits challenging the new statute that led to the District Court's decision. The Corporation also opposed the request for a Supreme Court stay of that decision, telling the Court in a memorandum that a stay would subject the Corporation to a grave and irreparable injury."

5. According to the above passage, it would be CORRECT to state that the Health and Hospitals Corporation

   A. joined Senator Ramsdell in his request for a stay
   B. opposed the statute which limited reimbursement for the cost of abortions
   C. claimed that it would experience a loss if the District Court order was enforced
   D. appealed the District Court decision

6. The above passage indicates that the Supreme Court acted in DIRECT response to

   A. a lawsuit initiated by the Health and Hospitals Corporation
   B. a ruling by a Federal District Court
   C. a request for a stay
   D. the passage of a new Federal statute

7. According to the above passage, it would be CORRECT to state that the Supreme Court

   A. blocked enforcement of the District Court order
   B. refused a request for a stay to block enforcement of the Federal statute
   C. ruled that the new Federal statute was unconstitutional
   D. permitted payment of Federal funds for abortion to continue

8. Following are three statements concerning abortion that might be correct: 8.____
    I. Abortion costs are no longer to be Federally reimbursed on the same basis as those for pregnancy and childbirth
    II. Federal funds have not been available for abortions except to save the life of the mother
    III. Medicaid has paid for elective abortions in the past

    According to the passage given above, which of the following CORRECTLY classifies the above statements into those that are true and those that are not true?

    A. I is true, but II and III are not.
    B. I and III are true, but II is not.
    C. I and II are true, but III is not.
    D. III is true, but I and II are not.

9. A legal memorandum will often include the following six sections: 9.____
    I. Conclusions
    II. Issues
    III. Analysis
    IV. Facts
    V. Unknowns
    VI. Counter-analysis

    Which of the following choices lists these sections in the sequence that is generally MOST appropriate for a legal memorandum?

    A. III, VI, IV, V, II, I   B. IV, II, III, VI, I, V
    C. V, II, IV, III, VI, I   D. II, IV, V, III, I, VI

Questions 10-13.

DIRECTIONS: Questions 10 through 13 consist of two sentences each. The sentences deal with the use of court opinions and cases in the writing of legal memoranda.
Select answer
   A. if only sentence I is correct
   B. if only sentence II is correct
   C. if both sentences are correct
   D. if neither sentence is correct

10. I. State the issues in the case as narrowly and precisely as possible. 10.____
    II. Quote frequently and at great length from the court opinions.

11. I. Describe briefly the issues in the case that are not related to your problem. 11.____
    II. Do not mention discrepancies between the facts of the case and the facts of your problem.

12. I. Do not refer to the holding or ruling in the case if it is harmful to your client. 12.____
    II. If the holding or ruling in the case is beneficial to your client, try to show that the facts of your problem are analogous to the facts of the case.

13. I. After stating your position concerning the issues and facts, present the opposite viewpoint as effectively as you can.
    II. Avoid stating your own opinions or conclusions concerning the applicability of the case.

14. Column V lists four publications in the legal field. Column W contains descriptions of basic subject matter of legal publications.
    Select the one of the following choices which BEST matches the publications in Column V with the subject matter in Column W.

    Column V
    I. Harvard Law Review
    II. Supreme Court Reporter
    III. McKinney's Consolidated Laws of New York
    IV. The Criminal Law Reporter

    Column W
    1. Law
    2. Commentary on law
    3. Combination of law and commentary

    A. I-3; II-1; III-2; IV-3
    B. I-2; II-3; III-2; IV-3
    C. I-2; II-1; III-3; IV-3
    D. I-2; II-3; III-3; IV-1

15. Tickler systems are used in many legal offices for scheduling and calendar control. Of the following, the LEAST common use of a tickler system is to

    A. keep papers filed in such a way that they may easily be retrieved
    B. arrange for the appearance of witnesses when they will be needed
    C. remind lawyers when certain papers are due
    D. arrange for the gathering of certain types of evidence

KEY (CORRECT ANSWERS)

1. B
2. B
3. A
4. C
5. B
6. C
7. D
8. D
9. B
10. A
11. D
12. B
13. A
14. C
15. A

TEST 2

DIRECTIONS: Each question or incomplete statement is followed by several suggested answers or completions. Select the one that BEST answers the question or completes the statement. *PRINT THE LETTER OF THE CORRECT ANSWER IN THE SPACE AT THE RIGHT.*

1. Studying the legislative history of a statute by reading the transcript of the hearings that were held on that subject is useful to the legal researcher PRIMARILY because it 1.____

   A. is informative of the manner in which laws are enacted
   B. helps him to understand the intent of the statute
   C. provides leads to statutes on the same subject
   D. clarifies the meaning of other statutes

2. Following are three statements concerning legal research that might be correct: 2.____
   I. The researcher may begin with a particular premise and, in researching it, may discover an entirely new approach to the problem
   II. When the researcher has located a relevant statute, it is not necessary to read court opinions interpreting or applying this statute
   III. A statute which is related to, but not the same as, the point being researched may have notes which will refer the researcher to more relevant cases

   Which of the following ACCURATELY classifies the above statements into those which are correct and those which are not?

   A. II and III are correct, but I is not.
   B. I and III are correct, but II is not.
   C. I and II are correct, but III is not.
   D. I, II, and III are all correct.

3. Of the following, the FIRST action a legal researcher should take in order to locate the laws relevant to a case is to 3.____

   A. search the index of a law book
   B. read statutes on similar subjects to discover pertinent annotations
   C. read a legal digest to become familiar with the law on the subject
   D. prepare a list of descriptive words applicable to the facts of the case

4. Which of the following is the BEST source for a legal researcher to consult in order to find historical data, cross-references, and case excerpts on cases, statutes, and regulations? 4.____

   A. Annotations   B. Digests
   C. Hornbooks   D. Casebooks

Questions 5-8.

DIRECTIONS: Each of Questions 5 through 8 contains two sentences concerning criminal law. Some of the sentences contain errors in English grammar or usage. A sentence does not contain an error simply because it could be written in a different manner. For each question, choose answer
   A. if only sentence I is correct
   B. if only sentence II is correct
   C. if both sentences are correct
   D. if neither sentence is correct

5. I. Limiting the term *property* to tangible property, in the criminal mischief setting, accords with prior case law holding that only tangible property came within the purview of the offense of malicious mischief.
   II. Thus, a person who intentionally destroys the property of another, but under an honest belief that he has title to such property, cannot be convicted of criminal mischief under the Revised Penal Law.

   5.____

6. I. Very early in it's history, New York enacted statutes from time to time punishing, either as a felony or as a misdemeanor, malicious injuries to various kinds of property: piers, booms, dams, bridges, etc.
   II. The application of the statute is necessarily restricted to trespassory takings with larcenous intent: namely with intent permanently or virtually permanently to *appropriate* property or *deprive* the owner of its use.

   6.____

7. I. Since the former Penal Law did not define the instruments of forgery in a general fashion, its crime of forgery was held to be narrower than the common law offense in this respect and to embrace only those instruments explicitly specified in the substantive provisions.
   II. After entering the barn through an open door for the purpose of stealing, it was closed by the defendants.

   7.____

8. I. The use of fire or explosives to destroy tangible property is proscribed by the criminal mischief provisions of the Revised Penal Law.
   II. The defendant's taking of a taxicab for the immediate purpose of affecting his escape did not constitute grand larceny

   8.____

Questions 9-13.

DIRECTIONS: Questions 9 through 13 are to be answered SOLELY on the basis of the following passage.

The law is quite clear that evidence obtained in violation of Section 605 of the Federal Communications Act is not admissible in federal court. However, the law as to the admissibility of evidence in state court is far from clear. Had the Supreme Court of the United States made the wiretap exclusionary rule applicable to the states, such confusion would not exist.

In the case of Alton v. Texas, the Supreme Court was called upon to determine whether wiretapping by state and local officers came within the proscription of the federal statute and, if so, whether Section 605 required the same remedies for its vindication in state courts. In answer to the first question, Mr. Justice Minton, speaking for the court, flatly stated that Section 605 made it a federal crime for anyone to intercept telephone messages and divulge what he learned. The court went on to say that a state officer who testified in state court concerning the existence, contents, substance, purport, effect or meaning of an intercepted conversation violated the federal law and committed a criminal act. In regard to the second question, however, the Supreme Court felt constrained by due regard for federal-state relations to answer in the negative. Mr. Justice Minton stated that the court would not presume, in the absence of a clear manifestation of congressional intent, that Congress intended to supersede state rules of evidence.

Because the Supreme Court refused to apply the exclusionary rule to wiretap evidence that was being used in state courts, the states respectively made this decision for themselves. According to hearings held before a congressional committee in 1975, six states authorize wiretapping by statute, 33 states impose total bans on wiretapping, and 11 states have no definite statute on the subject. For examples of extremes, a statute in Pennsylvania will be compared with a statute in New York.

The Pennsylvania statute provides that no communications by telephone or telegraph can be intercepted without permission of both parties. It also specifically prohibits such interception by public officials and provides that evidence obtained cannot be used in court.

The lawmakers in New York, recognizing the need for legal wiretapping, authorized wiretapping by statute. A New York law authorizes the issuance of an ex parte order upon oath or affirmation for limited wiretapping. The aim of the New York law is to allow court-ordered wiretapping and to encourage the testimony of state officers concerning such wiretapping in court. The New York law was found to be constitutional by the New York State Supreme Court in 1975. Other states, including Oregon, Maryland, Nevada, and Massachusetts, enacted similar laws which authorize court-ordered wiretapping.

To add to this legal disarray, the vast majority of the states, including New Jersey and New York, permit wiretapping evidence to be received in court even though obtained in violation of the state laws and of Section 605 of the Federal act. However, some states such as Rhode Island have enacted statutory exclusionary rules which provide that illegally procured wiretap evidence is incompetent in civil as well as criminal actions.

9. According to the above passage, a state officer who testifies in New York State court concerning the contents of a conversation he overheard through a court-ordered wiretap is in violation of _____ law.

    A. state law but not federal
    B. federal law but not state
    C. federal law and state
    D. neither federal nor state

10. According to the above passage, which of the following statements concerning states statutes on wiretapping is CORRECT?

    A. The number of states that impose total bans on wiretapping is three times as great as the number of states with no definite statute on wiretapping.
    B. The number of states having no definite statute on wiretapping is more than twice the number of states authorizing wiretapping.
    C. The number of states which authorize wiretapping by statute and the number of states having no definite statute on wiretapping exceed the number of states imposing total bans on wiretapping.
    D. More states authorize wiretapping by statute than impose total bans on wiretapping.

11. Following are three statements concerning wiretapping that might be valid:
    I. In Pennsylvania, only public officials may legally intercept telephone communications
    II. In Rhode Island, evidence obtained through an illegal wiretap is incompetent in criminal, but not civil, actions
    III. Neither Massachusetts nor Pennsylvania authorizes wiretapping by public officials

    According to the above passage, which of the following CORRECTLY classifies these statements into those that are valid and those that are not?

    A. I is valid, but II and III are not.
    B. II is valid, but I and III are not.
    C. II and III are valid, but I is not.
    D. None of the statements is valid.

12. According to the foregoing passage, evidence obtained in violation of Section 605 of the Federal Communications Act is inadmissible in

    A. federal court but not in any state courts
    B. federal court and all state courts
    C. all state courts but not in federal court
    D. federal court and some state courts

13. In regard to state rules of evidence, Mr. Justice Minton expressed the Court's opinion that Congress

    A. intended to supersede state rules of evidence, as manifested by Section 605 of the Federal Communications Act
    B. assumed that federal statutes would govern state rules of evidence in all wiretap cases
    C. left unclear whether it intended to supersede state rules of evidence
    D. precluded itself from superseding state rules of evidence through its regard for federal-state relations

14. You begin to ask follow-up questions of a witness who has given a statement. The witness starts to digress before answering an important question satisfactorily.
    In this situation, the BEST of the following steps is to

    A. guide the interview by suggesting answers to questions as they are asked
    B. ask questions which can be answered only with a simple *yes* or *no*
    C. construct questions as precisely as possible
    D. tell the witness to keep his answers brief

15. During an interview with a client, you have occasion to refer to a matter which is described in the legal profession by a technical term.
    Of the following, it would generally be MOST appropriate for you to

    A. discuss the underlying legal concept in detail
    B. avoid the subject since it is too complicated
    C. ask the client if he is familiar with the technical term
    D. describe the matter in everyday language

KEY (CORRECT ANSWERS)

1. B
2. B
3. D
4. A
5. C

6. B
7. A
8. A
9. B
10. A

11. D
12. D
13. C
14. C
15. D

EXAMINATION SECTION
TEST 1

DIRECTIONS: Each question or incomplete statement is followed by several suggested answers or completions. Select the one that BEST answers the question or completes the statement. *PRINT THE LETTER OF THE CORRECT ANSWER IN THE SPACE AT THE RIGHT.*

Questions 1-4.

DIRECTIONS: Questions 1 through 4 consist of sentences concerning criminal law. Some of the sentences contain errors in English grammar or usage, punctuation, spelling or capitalization. A sentence does not contain an error simply because it could be written in a different manner. Choose answer
- A. if the sentence contains an error in English grammar or usage
- B. if the sentence contains an error in punctuation
- C. if the sentence contains an error in spelling or capitalization
- D. if the sentence does not contain any errors

1. The severity of the sentence prescribed by contemporary statutes - including both the former and the revised New York Penal Laws - do not depend on what crime was intended by the offender. 1._____

2. It is generally recognized that two defects in the early law of attempt played a part in the birth of burglary: (1) immunity from prosecution for conduct short of the last act before completion of the crime, and (2) the relatively minor penalty imposed for an attempt (it being a common law misdemeanor) vis-a-vis the completed offense. 2._____

3. The first sentence of the statute is applicable to employees who enter their place of employment, invited guests, and all other persons who have an express or implied license or privilege to enter the premises. 3._____

4. Contemporary criminal codes in the United States generally divide burglary into various degrees, differentiating the categories according to place, time and other attentent circumstances. 4._____

Questions 5-8.

DIRECTIONS: Questions 5 through 8 are to be answered SOLELY on the basis of the following passage.

    The difficulty experienced in determining which party has the burden of proving payment or non-payment is due largely to a tack of consistency between the rules of pleading and the rules of proof. In some cases, a plaintiff is obligated by a rule of pleading to allege non-payment on his complaint, yet is not obligated to prove non-payment on the trial. An action upon a contract for the payment of money will serve as an illustration. In such a case, the plaintiff must allege non-payment in his complaint, but the burden of proving payment on the trial is upon the defendant. An important and frequently cited case on this problem is Conkling v. Weatherwax. In that case, the action was brought to establish and enforce a legacy as a lien upon real property. The defendant alleged in her answer that the legacy had been paid. There was no witness competent to testify for the plaintiff to show that the legacy had not been paid. Therefore, the question of the burden of proof became of primary importance since, if the plaintiff had the burden of proving non-payment, she must fail in her action; whereas, if the burden of proof was on the defendant to prove payment, the plaintiff might win. The Court of Appeals held that the burden of proof was on the plaintiff. In the course of his opinion, Judge Vann attempted to harmonize the conflicting cases on this subject, and for that purpose formulated three rules. These rules have been construed and applied to numerous subsequent cases. As so construed and applied, these may be summarized as follows:

Rule 1: In an action upon a contract for the payment of money only, where the complaint does not allege a balance due over and above all payments made, the plaintiff must allege nonpayment in his complaint, but the burden of proving payment is upon the defendant. In such a case, payment is an affirmative defense which the defendant must plead in his answer. If the defendant fails to plead payment, but pleads a general denial instead, he will not be permitted to introduce evidence of payment.

Rule 2: Where the complaint sets forth a balance in excess of all payments, owing to the structure of the pleading, burden is upon the plaintiff to prove his allegation. In this case, the defendant is not required to plead payment as a defense in his answer but may introduce evidence of payment under a general denial.

Rule 3: When the action is not upon contract for the payment of money, but is upon an obligation created by operation of law, or is for the enforcement of a lien where non-payment of the amount secured is part of the cause of action, it is necessary both to allege and prove the fact of nonpayment.

5. In the above passage, the case of Conkling v. Weatherwax was cited PRIMARILY to illustrate

    A. a case where the burden of proof was on the defendant to prove payment
    B. how the question of the burden of proof can affect the outcome of a case
    C. the effect of a legacy as a lien upon real property
    D. how conflicting cases concerning the burden of proof were harmonized

6. According to the above passage, the pleading of payment is a defense in

    A. Rule 1, but not Rules 2 and 3
    B. Rule 2, but not Rules 1 and 3
    C. Rules 1 and 3, but not Rule 2
    D. Rules 2 and 3, but not Rule 1

7. The facts in Conkling v. Weatherwax closely resemble the conditions described in Rule

    A. 1
    B. 2
    C. 3
    D. none of the rules

8. The major topic of the above passage may BEST be described as

    A. determining the ownership of property
    B. providing a legal definition
    C. placing the burden of proof
    D. formulating rules for deciding cases

Questions 9-12.

DIRECTIONS: Questions 9 through 12 consist of six sentences which can be arranged in a logical sequence. For each question, select the choice which places the numbered sentences in the MOST logical sequence.

9. I. The burden of proof as to each issue is determined before trial and remains upon the same party throughout the trial.
    II. The jury is at liberty to believe one witness testimony as against a number of contradictory witnesses.
    III. In a civil case, the party bearing the burden of proof is required to prove his contention by a fair preponderance of the evidence.
    IV. However, it must be noted that a fair preponderance of evidence does not necessarily mean a greater number of witnesses.
    V. The burden of proof is the burden which rests upon one of the parties to an action to persuade the trier of the facts, generally the jury, that a proposition he asserts is true.
    VI. If the evidence is equally balanced, or if it leaves the jury in such doubt as to be unable to decide the controversy either way, judgment must be given against the party upon whom the burden of proof rests.

    The CORRECT sequence is:

    A. III, II, V, IV, I, VI
    B. I, II, VI, V, III, IV
    C. III, IV, V, I, II, VI
    D. V, I, III, VI, IV, II

10. I. If a parent is without assets and is unemployed, he cannot be convicted of the crime of non-support of a child.
    II. The term *sufficient ability* has been held to mean sufficient financial ability.
    III. It does not matter if his unemployment is by choice or unavoidable circumstances.
    IV. If he fails to take any steps at all, he may be liable to prosecution for endangering the welfare of a child.
    V. Under the penal law, a parent is responsible for the support of his minor child only if the parent is of sufficient ability.
    VI. An indigent parent may meet his obligation by borrowing money or by seeking aid under the provisions of the Social Welfare Law.

    The CORRECT sequence is:

    A. VI, I, V, III, II, IV
    B. I, III, V, II, IV, VI
    C. V, II, I, III, VI, IV
    D. I, VI, IV, V, II, III

11.
 I. Consider, for example, the case of a rabble rouser who urges a group of twenty people to go out and break the windows of a nearby factory.
 II. Therefore, the law fills the indicated gap with the crime of *inciting to riot*.
 III. A person is considered guilty of inciting to riot when he urges ten or more persons to engage in tumultuous and violent conduct of a kind likely to create public alarm.
 IV. However, if he has not obtained the cooperation of at least four people, he cannot be charged with unlawful assembly.
 V. The charge of inciting to riot was added to the law to cover types of conduct which cannot be classified as either the crime of *riot* or the crime of *unlawful* assembly.
 VI. If he acquires the acquiescence of at least four of them, he is guilty of unlawful assembly even if the project does not materialize.

 The CORRECT sequence is:
 A. III, V, I, VI, IV, II
 B. V, I, IV, VI, II, III
 C. III, IV, I, V, II, VI
 D. V, I, IV, VI, III, II

12.
 I. If, however, the rebuttal evidence presents an issue of credibility, it is for the jury to determine whether the presumption has, in fact, been destroyed.
 II. Once sufficient evidence to the contrary is introduced, the presumption disappears from the trial.
 III. The effect of a presumption is to place the burden upon the adversary to come forward with evidence to rebut the presumption.
 IV. When a presumption is overcome and ceases to exist in the case, the fact or facts which gave rise to the presumption still remain.
 V. Whether a presumption has been overcome is ordinarily a question for the court.
 VI. Such information may furnish a basis for a logical inference.

 The CORRECT sequence is:
 A. IV, VI, II, V, I, III
 B. III, II, V, I, IV, VI
 C. V, III, VI, IV, II, I
 D. V, IV, I, II, VI, III

13. In order to obtain an accurate statement from a person who has witnessed a crime, it is BEST to question the witness

 A. as soon as possible after the crime was committed
 B. after the witness has discussed the crime with other witnesses
 C. after the witness has had sufficient time to reflect on events and formulate a logical statement
 D. after the witness has been advised that he is obligated to tell the whole truth

14. A young woman was stabbed in the hand in her home by her estranged boyfriend. Her mother and two sisters were at home at the time.
 Of the following, it would generally be BEST to interview the young woman in the presence of

 A. her mother only
 B. all members of her immediate family
 C. members of the family who actually observed the crime
 D. the official authorities

15. The one of the following which is NOT effective in obtaining complete testimony from a witness during an interview is to   15._____

    A. ask questions in chronological order
    B. permit the witness to structure the interview
    C. make sure you fully understand the response to each question
    D. review questions to be asked beforehand

KEY (CORRECT ANSWERS)

1. A   6. A
2. D   7. C
3. D   8. C
4. C   9. D
5. B   10. C

11. A
12. B
13. A
14. D
15. B

TEST 2

DIRECTIONS: Each question or incomplete statement is followed by several suggested answers or completions. Select the one that BEST answers the question or completes the statement. *PRINT THE LETTER OF THE CORRECT ANSWER IN THE SPACE AT THE RIGHT.*

1. You are conducting an initial interview with a witness who expresses reluctance, even hostility, to being questioned. You feel it would be helpful to take some notes during the interview.
   In this situation, it would be BEST to

   A. put off note-taking until a follow-up interview and concentrate on establishing rapport with the witness
   B. explain the necessity of note-taking and proceed to take notes during the interview
   C. make notes from memory after the witness has left
   D. take notes, but as unobtrusively as possible

   1.____

2. An assistant is starting an interview with an elderly man who was the victim of a robbery. The man begins by mentioning his minor aches and pains. The aide immediately changes the subject to the robbery.
   This action by the aide should GENERALLY be considered

   A. *proper* chiefly because it speeds up the interviewing process
   B. *improper* chiefly because the man is likely to become confused as to what information is really important
   C. *proper* chiefly because the man is likely to be impressed with the aide's interest in the crime
   D. *improper* chiefly because an opportunity for gaining pertinent information may be lost

   2.____

3. You are interviewing the owner of a stolen car about facts relating to the robbery. After completing his statement, the car owner suddenly states that some of the details he has just related are not correct. You realize that this change might be significant.
   Of the following, it would be BEST for you to

   A. ask the owner what other details he may have given incorrectly
   B. make a note of the discrepancy for discussion at a later date
   C. repeat your questioning on the details that were misstated until you have covered that area completely
   D. explain to the owner that because of his change of testimony, you will have to repeat the entire interview

   3.____

4. You are interviewing a client who has just been assaulted. He has trouble collecting his thoughts and telling his story coherently.
   Which of the following represents the MOST effective method of questioning under these circumstances?

   A. Ask questions which structure the client's story chronologically into units, each with a beginning, middle, and end.
   B. Ask several questions at a time to structure the interview.

   4.____

C. Ask open-ended questions which allow the client to respond in a variety of ways.
D. Begin the interview with several detailed questions in order to focus the client's attention on the situation.

5. Following are two statements that might be correct concerning the relationship with clients:

   I. When practical the client should be encouraged to take some steps on his own behalf to aid the office in handling his case
   II. The client should be told what steps the office proposes to take on his behalf

   Which of the following CORRECTLY classifies the above statements?

   A. Statement I is generally correct, but Statement II is not.
   B. Statement II is generally correct, but Statement I is not.
   C. Both statements are generally correct.
   D. Neither statement is generally correct.

6. You are in the District Attorney's office interviewing an elderly female victim of an assault in order to prepare a list of charges.
   The one of the following which would be MOST important in determining all the facts is

   A. creating a close, cooperative working relationship with the victim
   B. establishing your authority at the beginning of the interview
   C. maintaining a relaxed atmosphere during the interview
   D. having access to the particular statutes which might apply to this case

7. A client is critical of the way he has been treated by government agencies in the past. A paralegal aide interviewing him defends the overall performance of government employees.
   This reaction by the aide is GENERALLY

   A. *appropriate;* the aide has an obligation to defend fellow workers in government service when such defense is justified
   B. *inappropriate;* the aide should remain neutral rather than volunteer his personal opinions
   C. *appropriate;* the aide should honestly express his personal opinions in such circumstances unless it is likely to provoke antagonism
   D. *inappropriate;* the aide should agree with the client's comments to help establish a greater rapport with him

Questions 8-11.

DIRECTIONS: Questions 8 through 11 are to be answered SOLELY on the basis of the following passage.

A person may use physical force upon another person when and to the extent he reasonably believes such to be necessary to defend himself or a third person from what he reasonably believes to be the use or imminent use of unlawful physical force by such other person, unless (a) the latter's conduct was provoked by the actor himself with intent to cause physical injury to another person, or (b) the actor was the initial aggressor; or (c) the physical force involved is the product of a combat by agreement not specifically authorized by law.

A person may not use deadly physical force upon another person under the circumstances specified above unless: (a) he reasonably believes that such other person is using or is about to use deadly physical force. Even in such case, however, the actor may not use deadly physical force if he knows he can with complete safety as to himself and others avoid the necessity of doing so by retreating, except that he is under no duty to retreat if he is in his dwelling and is not the initial aggressor; or (b) he reasonably believes that such other person is committing or attempting to commit a kidnapping, forcible rape, or forcible sodomy.

8. Jones and Smith, who have not met before, get into an argument in a tavern. Smith takes a punch at Jones but misses. Jones then hits Smith on the chin with his fist. Smith falls to the floor and suffers minor injuries. According to the above passage, it would be CORRECT to state that

   A. *only* Smith was justified in using physical force
   B. *only* Jones was justified in using physical force
   C. both Smith and Jones were justified in using physical force
   D. neither Smith nor Jones was justified in using physical force

9. While walking down the street, Brady observes Miller striking Mrs. Adams on the head with his fist in an attempt to steal her purse.
   According to the above passage, it would be CORRECT to state that Brady would

   A. not be justified in using deadly physical force against Miller since Brady can safety retreat
   B. be justified in using physical force against Miller, but not deadly physical force
   C. not be justified in using physical force against Miller since Brady himself is not being attacked
   D. be justified in using deadly physical force

10. Winters is attacked from behind by Sharp, who attempts to beat up Winters with a blackjack. Winters disarms Sharp and succeeds in subduing him with a series of blows to the head. Sharp stops fighting and explains that he thought Winters was the person who had robbed his apartment a few minutes before, but now realizes his mistake. According to the above passage, it would be CORRECT to state that

    A. Winters was justified in using physical force on Sharp only to the extent necessary to defend himself
    B. Winters was not justified in using physical force on Sharp since Sharp's attack was provoked by what he believed to be Winters' behavior
    C. Sharp was justified in using physical force on Winters since he reasonably believed that Winters had unlawfully robbed him
    D. Winters was justified in using physical force on Sharp only because Sharp was acting mistakenly in attacking him

11. Roberts hears a noise in the cellar of his home and, upon investigation, discovers an intruder, Welch. Welch moves towards Roberts in a threatening manner, thrusts his hand into a bulging pocket, and withdraws what appears to be a gun. Roberts thereupon strikes Welch over the head with a golf club. He then sees that the *gun* is a toy. Welch later dies of head injuries.
    According to the above passage, it would be CORRECT to state that Roberts

A. *was justified* in using deadly physical force because he reasonably believed Welch was about to use deadly physical force
B. *was not justified* in using deadly physical force
C. *was justified* in using deadly physical force only because he did not provoke Welch's conduct
D. *was justified* in using deadly physical force only because he was not the initial aggressor

Questions 12-15.

DIRECTIONS: Questions 12 through 15 are to be answered SOLELY on the basis of the following passage.

From the beginning, the Supreme Court has supervised the fairness of trials conducted by the Federal government. But the Constitution, as originally drafted, gave the court no such general authority in state oases. The court's power to deal with state cases comes from the Fourteenth Amendment, which became part of the Constitution in 1868. The crucial provision forbids any state to "deprive any person of life, liberty or property without due process of law."

The guarantee of "due process" would seem, at the least, to require fair procedure in criminal trials. But curiously, the Supreme Court did not speak on the question for many decades. During that time, however, the due process clause was interpreted to bar "unreasonable" state economic regulations, such as minimum wage laws.

In 1915, there came the case of Leo M. Frank, a Georgian convicted of murder in a trial that he contended was dominated by mob hysteria. Historians now agree that there was such hysteria, with overtones of anti-semitism.

The Supreme Court held that it could not look past the findings of the Georgia courts that there had been no mob atmosphere at the trial. Justices Oliver Wendell Holmes and Charles Evans Hughes dissented, arguing that the constitutional guarantee would be "a barren one" if the Federal courts could not make their own inferences from the facts.

In 1923, the case of Moore v. Dempsey involved five Arkansas blacks convicted of murder and sentenced to death in a community so aroused against them that at one point they were saved from lynching only by Federal troops. Witnesses against them were said to have been beaten into testifying.

The court, though not actually setting aside the convictions, directed a lower Federal court to hold a habeas corpus hearing to find out whether the trial had been fair, or whether the whole proceeding had been "a mask — that counsel, jury, and judge were swept to the fatal end by an irresistible wave of public opinion."

12. According to the above passage, the Supreme Court's INITIAL interpretation of the Fourteenth Amendment

    A. protected state supremacy in economic matters
    B. increased the scope of Federal jurisdiction
    C. required fair procedures in criminal trials
    D. prohibited the enactment of minimum wage laws

12.____

13. According to the above passage, the Supreme Court in the Frank case

    A. denied that there had been mob hysteria at the trial
    B. decided that the guilty verdict was supported by the evidence
    C. declined to question the state court's determination of the facts
    D. found that Leo Frank had not received *due process*

14. According to the above passage, the dissenting judges in the Frank case maintained that

    A. due process was an empty promise in the circumstances of that case
    B. the Federal courts could not guarantee certain provisions of the Constitution
    C. the Federal courts should not make their own inferences from the facts in state cases
    D. the Supreme Court had rendered the Constitution *barren*

15. Of the following, the MOST appropriate title for the above passage is:

    A. THE CONDUCT OF FEDERAL TRIALS
    B. THE DEVELOPMENT OF STATES' RIGHTS: 1868-1923
    C. MOORE V. DEMPSEY: A CASE STUDY IN CRIMINAL JUSTICE
    D. DUE PROCESS - THE EVOLUTION OF A CONSTITUTIONAL CORNERSTONE

KEY (CORRECT ANSWERS)

1. B
2. D
3. C
4. A
5. C

6. A
7. B
8. B
9. B
10. A

11. A
12. D
13. C
14. A
15. D

EXAMINATION SECTION
TEST 1

DIRECTIONS: Each question or incomplete statement is followed by several suggested answers or completions. Select the one that BEST answers the question or completes the statement. *PRINT THE LETTER OF THE CORRECT ANSWER IN THE SPACE AT THE RIGHT.*

Questions 1-11.

DIRECTIONS: Questions 1 through 11 are to be answered SOLELY on the basis of the following passage.

KELSEN AND THE PURE THEORY OF LAW

Kelsen is the founder and storm center of a school of juristic theory known from its place of origin as the "Vienna School of Jurisprudence" and from its point of view as the "normative theory of law" and the "pure theory of law." His ideas have met with a great deal of opposition and the polemics have been conducted with so much vehemence and passion that, as Kelsen himself says, there is grave suspicion that the motives on the side of the opposition have not been purely theoretical or scientific. According to Kelsen, his opponents could not forgive him for endeavoring to establish a purely formal science of law and of the state which could not be used as a tool in the service of political interests. His general criticism of the prevailing theories is that they are not purely juristic, but political. Jurisprudence has been used as a weapon of defense or attack, with a view to justifying or condemning a form of government or a legal order. This being the situation, particularly in central Europe, a political motive has been sought in Kelsen's theory also. Fascists have seen in it a defense of democratic liberalism; liberals and social democrats have regarded it as paving the way to Fascism. Communists find in it capitalistic ideology, while the conservatives accuse it of sheer Bolshevism or concealed anarchism. Its spirit has been compared with that of Catholic Scholasticism, Protestantism, and even atheism. Sure proof, Kelsen says, that it is in reality what it claims to be -- none of these, having, as a pure formal science of law, no political or theological implications.

Kelsen carefully prepares the ground in a discussion of the place of jurisprudence among the sciences. He divides the sciences into natural and normative. The natural sciences deal with "Being" and consist in explaining "Being." To explain natural phenomena means to present them as illustrations of the law of causality. A normative science is one which studies the structure or form of the norm, not its content. It is, therefore, a formal science. A norm is distinguished from a natural law. A natural law states a causal relation between "being" and "being" and thus explains "Being." A norm also states a relation between "being" and "Being." The "Being" in this case is in the majority of instances a human act. But the relation in this case is not one of cause and effect, but one of "ought." The norm establishes a duty; it does not explain. "Being" and "ought" are two primary categories of thought. They cannot be defined and are independent of each other. Neither can be derived from the other.

Attempts have been made, Kelsen points out, to reduce norms to natural law. Thus, it is said that moral norms are in effect precipitates of that which a given society or mankind in general have actually been observing for a long time. Kelsen's answer to this is that while it may be true that, psychologically, long habit has the tendency to create in the human mind a *feeling that the act in question ought to be observed, it is a confusion of thought to identify the "ought" category with the habit which produced it.*

It has been maintained likewise that the norm: "Thou shalt not lie" is only another way of saying: "Lying has a tendency to destroy social confidence," and the latter is a natural law like the proposition: "Alcohol has a tendency to destroy the nervous system." This too is the result of a confusion between the norm which established the duty and the ground in natural law which prompted moralists to establish the norm. Thus, so far as meaning is concerned, norm and natural law are always different.

Thus, Kelsen distinguishes jurisprudence as a normative science separate and distinct from natural sciences. Although there are many kinds of norms, norms of ethics, aesthetics, grammar, logic, law, Kelsen is primarily interested in legal norms. Kelsen has formulated what he calls the primary legal norm. The primary legal norm has the form of a conditional sentence or a hypothetical judgment: "If A steals, he should be punished." The act of stealing is, therefore, not a violation of a norm; it is precisely in connection with the act of stealing that the legal norm becomes effective. Hence, it is a mistake to regard the law as an expression of what people think, or do, or observe. The normative method is here entirely separate from the explicative, and the jurist is concerned primarily with the normative aspect. To be sure, this is only one aspect of law, and does not enable us to comprehend fully the institution or phenomenon of law. The jurist may and should carry on sociological, psychological, and historical studies of the law, but he should not mix these studies, which are explicative, with the formal -- juristic -- normative. These studies do not constitute a psychological or sociological jurisprudence -- there is no such thing, says Kelsen. They are the psychology or sociology of law or of human conduct in relation to law. The theoretical jurist is not interested in the actual behavior of men, but in the "ought" which the law prescribes. His criteria are purely formal like those of the judge.

Of course, moral as well as legal norms determine an "ought." Kelsen feels that a jurist presupposes a given body of law, be its origin what it may, and as he is not interested in the origin so he is not concerned with its purpose, though there is no doubt that legal norms have been established for a purpose. This purpose, however, has no bearing on the meaning of the concepts based upon the norms. He considers legal concepts purely as formal categories and hence admits only formal elements in his definitions. By way of example, geometry is none the less an important and useful science because it considers only the form of bodies; and the same is true of jurisprudence.

Kelsen feels that his pure theory of law is neither the dogmatic jurisprudence which develops a certain juridical order by studying a group of norms or analyzing a particular rule of law in order to make their meaning more precise, nor the history of law which attempts to study the historical origins of a particular juridical order, nor the comparative law which attempts to compare the contents of various juridical orders, looking for conformity or diversity, in order to arrive at certain juridical types, but that of general jurisprudence. This latter, Kelsen says, is a jurisprudence that does not restrict itself to a particular juridical order or to particular rules. The task of such a jurisprudence, therefore, constitutes the theoretical basis for all other branches of jurisprudence.

1. The *normative theory of law* is   1.____

A. frequently mistaken for a theory called the *pure theory of law*
B. synonymous with the *pure theory of law*
C. the storm center of the Vienna School of Jurisprudence
D. largely polemical

2. Kelsen maintains that the *normative theory* 2.____

   A. is a pure science of law having no political or theological implications
   B. must be understood in order to establish the validity of legal systems in a democracy
   C. is meant to be atheistic since there is no reference to an external moral code
   D. supports several different political positions

3. Which one of the following statements is NOT correct? 3.____

   A. Kelsen believes his attackers are not interested in a purely juristic theory of law.
   B. Kelsen criticizes legal theories which are designed to serve political purposes.
   C. Kelsen believes that most jurisprudential theories are used to justify or attack a given form of government.
   D. Kelsen's theories have been accepted by a wide spectrum of political theorists from left to right.

4. Which of the following is the basis of Kelsen's theory of jurisprudence? 4.____

   A. Pure philosophical models
   B. Differences between natural and normative sciences
   C. A geometric model having axioms and postulates
   D. Sociological concepts

5. According to the passage, it would be CORRECT to state that a normative science 5.____

   A. defines cause and effect
   B. explains natural law
   C. examines *being* and what ought to follow
   D. establishes the interdependency of *being* and *duty*

6. According to the passage, it would be CORRECT to state that natural science 6.____

   A. is one category of normative science
   B. studies the structure and form of the norm
   C. is mistakenly believed to explain natural phenomena
   D. deals with and explains *being*

7. Which one of the following statements concerning norms and natural law is NOT correct? 7.____

   A. The universality of a given standard of conduct indicates that it is a true natural law.
   B. Norms cannot be reduced to natural law since the two are not the same.
   C. The equation of natural law with norms arises from the confusion between things that have been done out of habit and things that ought to be done.
   D. *Thou shalt not lie* is an example of a norm.

8. According to the passage, it would be CORRECT to state that Kelsen's primary legal norm 8.____

A. is an expression of what people do
B. permits a full comprehension of law as an institution
C. defines an illegal act as the violation of a norm
D. takes the form of a hypothetical judgement

9. According to Kelsen, which one of the following statement is NOT correct? 9.____

   A. Jurist is concerned primarily with the normative aspect of law.
   B. Sociological and psychological studies of the law do not constitute a separate jurisprudence.
   C. The theoretical jurist is concerned with the actual behavior of men in relation to the norms which the law prescribes.
   D. The normative and explicative methods are entirely different from each other.

10. A jurist concerned with legal norms considers 10.____

    A. legal concepts in terms of purely formal criteria
    B. whether the *ought* of the legal category conforms to the *ought* of the moral category
    C. the origins of any given body of law
    D. the purpose of a body of law in determining the meaning of concepts based upon its norms

11. According to the passage, it would be CORRECT to state that the pure theory of law 11.____

    A. is instrumental in the development of comparative jurisprudential analyses
    B. constitutes the theoretical basis for all other branches of jurisprudence
    C. establishes a body of dogma for the guidance of jurists
    D. clarifies the meaning of particular rules of law

12. Trees which grow annually on reality are considered 12.____

    A. real property   B. personal property
    C. accretions   D. avulsions

13. Where is a grant of a fee simple is to John Jones and Jones, his wife, the grantees take as 13.____

    A. tenants in common   B. individuals
    C. joint tenants   D. tenants by the entirety

14. Assume that A and B are joint tenants of realty. A conveys his share of the realty absolutely to C, without the knowledge or consent of B. 14.____
    With regard of C's status under these circumstances, it would be CORRECT to state that C

    A. becomes a joint tenant with B
    B. takes nothing, and A remains a joint tenant with B
    C. takes nothing, and A becomes a tenant in common with B
    D. becomes a tenant in common with B as to that part of the realty conveyed to him

15. Assume that two persons own a piece of realty as tenants in common. One of them, without the consent of the other, takes possession of the realty and claims openly to hold adversely to the other. 15.____
    Such possession, at its start, is deemed to be

A. adverse possession
B. the possession of the other
C. constructive possession
D. adverse possession only if the property is income-producing

16. Assume that a fee owner conveys a portion of his realty to another, while keeping other land to which he has no access except by passing over the land conveyed.
With regard to the grantor's access to the property he retains, it would be CORRECT to state that

   A. an easement by prescription inures to the benefit of the grantor
   B. an easement is reserved by implication if at the time of the conveyance it would result in a mere convenience
   C. an easement is reserved by implication if actual necessity exists at the time of the conveyance
   D. no easement exists unless it is stipulated in the instrument conveying the realty

17. Assume that A owns a piece of realty and enters into a valid contract to sell the same to X for a purchase price of $50,000, all cash. Before the closing of title, A dies, leaving a valid will which leaves all of his realty to B and all of his personalty to C.
With regard to conveyance of the realty, it would be CORRECT to state that

   A. there is no legal duty on anyone's part to execute the conveyance in accordance with the contract
   B. the property must be conveyed with the proceeds going to B
   C. the property must be conveyed with the proceeds going to C
   D. the property must be conveyed with the proceeds shared equally between B and C as a matter of law

18. The statute of limitations in an action on a note which is secured by a mortgage on real property is _____ years.

   A. 3   B. 6   C. 10   D. 20

19. Assume that a written lease has been validly assigned by a tenant to an assignee. The lease contains a renewal option in favor of the tenant but is silent as to the rights there to of assignees.
With regard to the assignee's rights, it would be CORRECT to state that the

   A. assignee may compel the landlord to renew the lease to the assignor
   B. assignment terminated the renewal option
   C. assignee has no rights of any kind with respect to the renewal option
   D. rights of the assignee with respect to the renewal option depend on whether the assignee assumed the obligations of the lease

20. Assume that an employee, after returning home from work, told his wife that he had injured himself on the job that afternoon while lifting some heavy objects. The employee had suffered from chest pains since the lifting incident and thereafter died of a heart attack. The wife subsequently seeks benefits at a Workmen's Compensation hearing.
With regard to the admissibility of the employee's statement to his wife at such a hearing, it would be CORRECT to state that the statement is

A. inadmissible as a matter of law
B. admissible as a matter of law without regard to any other facts
C. inadmissible solely because of the hearsay rule
D. admissible if corroborated by other evidence

21. Substantial evidence, as required to confirm the finding of an administrative agency on judicial review, is

A. evidence beyond a reasonable doubt
B. such relevant evidence as a reasonable mind might accept as adequate to support a conclusion
C. a mere scintilla of evidence
D. a preponderance of the evidence

22. Assume that a municipal contractor is suing the city to recover the balance due on a contract. The contractor had previously been convicted in Federal Court of using interstate facilities with intent to violate the state bribery laws in connection with said contract, and the city counter claims for recovery of the payments already made.
If there is no basis for determining the damages that the city has sustained, who should recover?

A. The contractor is entitled to the balance due.
B. The city is entitled to recover the payments it has made.
C. The contractor is entitled to quantum merit.
D. Neither party is entitled to anything.

23. Assume that the estate of a deceased motorcyclist is bringing an action against a town for negligence in the maintenance of a bridge abutment. The decedent died in an accident when the motorcycle he was driving crashed into the abutment. Immediately after the accident, the coroner ordered an autopsy and blood and urine tests to determine the alcoholic content of the decedent at the time of his death, pursuant to a state statute. Under these circumstances, what action should the court take with regard to the evidence derived from the autopsy and blood and urine tests?
The court should

A. bar the admission of the alcohol analysis into evidence on the grounds that the statute is unconstitutional
B. allow the defendant town to introduce into evidence that part of the autopsy report which contains the alcohol analysis
C. bar the admission into evidence by the town that part of the autopsy report which contains the alcohol analysis
D. allow the alcohol analysis to be introduced in evidence only if the coroner appears to testify

24. Assume that, in a criminal case, a defendant bookseller is charged with possession and sale of an obscene magazine. At the trial, the magazine itself is found to be obscene. Under these circumstances, what presumption, if any, concerning the bookseller's knowledge should apply?

A. There is a valid statutory presumption that a seller of obscene materials knows the contents of what he sells.
B. There is no statutory presumption that a seller of obscene materials knows the contents of what he sells.

C. No presumptions of any kind arise by virtue of the fact that a defendant possessed and sold obscene materials.
D. Actual knowledge of the contents of obscene materials must be proved against the seller.

25. Assume that a plaintiff institutes an action in damages against D and C alleging them to be joint tort feasors whose negligence was the sole cause of his injury, and both D and C appear at the trial.
Under these circumstances, which of the following is a PROPER action for the jury to take?
The jury

　　A. *must,* if it finds for the plaintiff, bring in a single verdict against D and C
　　B. *can,* if it finds for the plaintiff, exonerate both D and C and bring in a verdict against X, who is not a party to this action
　　C. *can,* if it finds for the plaintiff, apportion the damages between D and C
　　D. *can,* if it desires to find for the plaintiff, waive any contributory negligence of the plaintiff but reduce his verdict against D and C

25.____

KEY (CORRECT ANSWERS)

1.	B	11.	B
2.	A	12.	A
3.	D	13.	D
4.	B	14.	D
5.	C	15.	B
6.	D	16.	C
7.	A	17.	C
8.	D	18.	B
9.	C	19.	A
10.	A	20.	D

21.	B
22.	B
23.	C
24.	A
25.	C

TEST 2

DIRECTIONS: Each question or incomplete statement is followed by several suggested answers or completions. Select the one that BEST answers the question or completes the statement. *PRINT THE LETTER OF THE CORRECT ANSWER IN THE SPACE AT THE RIGHT.*

Questions 1-10.

DIRECTIONS: Questions 1 through 10 are to be answered SOLELY on the basis of the following sections of the General Business Law.

§200. Safes; limited liability

Whenever the proprietor or manager of any hotel, motel, inn or steamboat shall provide a safe in the office of such hotel, motel or steamboat, or other convenient place for the safe keeping of any money, jewels, ornaments, bank notes, bonds, negotiable securities or precious stones belonging to the guests of or travelers in such hotel, motel, inn or steamboat, and shall notify the guests or travelers thereof by posting a notice stating the fact that such safe is provided, in which such property may be deposited, in a public and conspicuous place and manner in the office and public rooms, and in the public parlors of such hotel, motel, or inn, or saloon of such steam boat, and if such guest or traveller shall neglect to deliver such property, to the person in charge of such office for deposit in such safe, the proprietor or manager of such hotel, motel, or steamboat shall not be liable for any loss of such property, sustained by such guest or traveler by theft or otherwise; but no hotel, motel or steamboat proprietor, manager or lessee shall be obliged to receive property on deposit for safe keeping, exceeding five hundred dollars in value; and if such guest or traveler shall deliver such property to the person in charge of such office for deposit in such safe, said proprietor, manager or lessee shall not be liable for any loss thereof, sustained by such guest or traveler by theft or otherwise, in any sum exceeding the sum of five hundred dollars unless by special agreement in writing with such proprietor, manager or lessee.

§201. Liability for loss of clothing and other personal property limited

1. No hotel or motel keeper except as provided in the foregoing section shall be liable for damage to or loss of wearing apparel or other personal property in the lobby, hallways or in the room or rooms assigned to a guest for any sum exceeding the sum of five hundred dollars, unless it shall appear that such loss occurred through the fault or negligence of such keeper, nor shall he be liable in any sum exceeding the sum of one hundred dollars for the loss of or damage to any such property when delivered to such keeper for storage or safe keeping in the store room, baggage room or other place elsewhere than in the room or rooms assigned to such guest, unless at the time of delivering the same for storage or safe keeping such value in excess of one hundred dollars shall be stated and a written receipt, stating such value, shall be issued by such keeper, but in no event shall such keeper be liable beyond five hundred dollars, unless it shall appear that such loss occurred through his fault or negligence, and such keeper may make a reasonable charge for storing or keeping such property, nor shall he be liable for the loss of or damage to any merchandise samples or merchandise for sale, unless the guest shall have given such keeper prior written notice of having the same in his possession, together with the value thereof, the receipt of which notice the hotel or motel keeper shall acknowledge in writing over the signature of himself or his agent, but in no event shall such keeper be liable beyond five hundred dollars, unless it shall appear that such loss or damage occurred through his fault or negligence; as to property deposited by guests or patrons in the parcel or check room of any hotel, motel or restaurant, the delivery of which is evidenced by a check or receipt therefor and for which no fee or charge is exacted, the proprietor shall not be liable beyond seventy-five dollars, unless such value in excess of seventy-five dollars shall be stated upon delivery and a written receipt, stating such value, shall be issued, but he shall in no event be liable beyond one hundred dollars, unless such loss occurs through his fault or negligence. Notwithstanding anything here in above contained, no hotel or motel keeper shall be liable for damage to or loss of such property by fire, when it shall appear that such fire was occasioned without his fault or negligence.

2. A printed copy of this section shall be posted in a conspicuous place and manner in the office or public room and in the public parlors of such hotel or motel.

1. Which one of the following statements concerning Section 200 is NOT correct?

   A. The section is applicable to hotels, motels and steamboats.
   B. It provides a method whereby the covered places of public accommodation may limit their liability for losses of specified valuables.
   C. It mandates the provision of a safe for the deposit of valuables for all hotels, motels and steamboats.
   D. The provisions of this section apply to the valuables of guests and travelers only.

2. According to the passage, it would be CORRECT to state that if a hotel provides a safe for specified valuables under the conditions specified in Section 200,

   A. its liability for losses is limited to $500
   B. it may refuse to receive property that is more valuable than $500
   C. its liability is limited to $1,000 unless the guest declares the value to be greater and the manager, proprietor or lessee agrees in writing to accept a higher valuation
   D. it is liable up to a limit of $500 for losses arising only from thefts

3. According to the passage, if a hotel complies with all the requirements of Section 200, and a guest fails to deposit designated valuables in the hotel safe, the guest

   A. *cannot* hold the public place liable under any circumstances for losses sustained
   B. *can* hold the public place liable only if the property is stolen
   C. *cannot* hold the public place liable unless he can prove the loss occurred through the negligence of the management
   D. *can* hold the management of the public place liable for any loss not in excess of $500

4. Section 201 of the General Business Law establishes the liability of hotels and motels for clothing(,)

   A. and/or other personal property and valuables stolen from the guest's assigned room
   B. personal property and valuables lost from any cause within the hotel or motel
   C. or personal property, except valuables or merchandise samples or merchandise for sale, which is stolen or otherwise lost
   D. or other personal property, except valuables, lost or stolen from designed areas within the hotel or motel

5. Under Section 201, liability for clothing or other personal property therein designated, with the exception of merchandise, which is lost, stolen or otherwise damaged while in the assigned room is

   A. *limited* to $500 regardless of the cause of the loss
   B. *limited* to $500 if the loss is caused by the management's negligence
   C. *unlimited* under any circumstances
   D. *unlimited* if due to the negligence of the management

5.____

6. Which one of the following provisions is NOT applicable to property that is stored?

   A. The limitations on storage apply only to property stored in storage or baggage rooms and not to property stored in the assigned room.
   B. The limitations on liability for storage areas are applicable only if no storage charge is made.
   C. The hotel or motel is liable in amounts over $100 only if an excess valuation is declared and a written receipt issued.
   D. There is a maximum liability of $500 provided, unless loss is due to the negligence or fault of the management.

6.____

7. A travelling salesman having merchandise samples or other merchandise for sale in his room

   A. keeps it there at his own risk
   B. can obtain limited coverage for loss by insuring it with the hotel or motel, which must provide such insurance or coverage at a fee
   C. may recover for any loss in any amount if the loss is due to the fault or negligence of the hotel or motel keeper
   D. will obtain coverage for loss by notifying the management in advance that he will have the property with him, and its value

7.____

8. Certain provisions of Section 201 apply to

   A. all parcel and check rooms
   B. parcel and check rooms in restaurants that do not charge a fee but do issue checks
   C. parcel and check rooms in hotels and motels, and restaurants in such hotels and motels
   D. only to parcel and check rooms that charge fees in hotels, motels and restaurants

8.____

9. The limit of liability for parcel and check rooms covered by this section is

   A. $75 if no excess valuation is declared and the loss is not due to negligence or fault on the part of the management
   B. $75 if no excess valuation is declared, but up to the lost property's full value if an excess valuation is declared and accepted by the management as evidenced by a written receipt
   C. $75 if no excess valuation is declared and $100 if an excess valuation is declared and the loss arises from the negligence or fault of the management
   D. $100 regardless of the circumstances of the loss

9.____

10. Generally, liability encompassed under Section 201 EXCLUDES losses

10.____

A. occasioned by fires not due to negligence
B. arising out of the management's negligence
C. for property not placed in a storage room, baggage room, parcel or check room, or in the hotel or motel safe
D. for stored property unless a check or receipt is given therefor

11. Assume that P has been injured as a result of the negligence of joint tort feasors D and C.
As part of his action to recover damages, P

    A. must join D and C as defendants
    B. has the right to name only D as a defendant
    C. has the right to name only D as a defendant, but only after he has settled with C
    D. is barred from any settlement before trial with either D or C

12. Assume that A was driving a car in a northerly direction and that B was driving a car along the same road in a southerly direction. B's car crashed into A's car solely as the result of a defective steering mechanism in B's car, for which B could have brought a breach of warranty of merchantability action against the manufacturer of the car.
What are A's right under these circumstances?

    A. A's only remedy is against B in negligence.
    B. A has no cause of action in breach of warranty against the manufacturer of B's car unless A and B are in privity with each other.
    C. A's only remedy against the manufacturer of B's car is in negligence.
    D. A has a cause of action in breach of warranty against the manufacturer of B's car.

13. Assume that a mother negligently walks her 10-year-old child across the street against the light, and the child is injured while crossing by the negligent operation of D's auto.
It would be CORRECT to state that, in an action by the child against D for personal injuries,

    A. the child of this age can not be guilty of negligence as a matter of law
    B. there is a rebuttable presumption that the child was also negligent
    C. the negligence of the mother is not imputed to the child
    D. the child in this case would have to prove that D was guilty of willful misconduct

14. Assume that P, while a patient in X Hospital, suffers personal injuries as the result of the medical malpractice of D, a staff physician of X Hospital.
Under these circumstances, who is liable if P brings an action to recover for said injuries?

    A. Only D is liable for negligence.
    B. X Hospital is liable for negligence.
    C. X Hospital is liable only for administrative negligence.
    D. D is liable only for willful negligence.

15. Assume that F negligently operates his auto so as to cause an accident with another car resulting in personal injuries to his son P, a passenger in F's car.
If P's injuries exceed the no-fault threshold, P

A. can recover for his personal injuries only against the driver of the other car involved in the accident
B. has no cause of action against F
C. has a cause of action against F only if he can prove willful misconduct on F's part
D. has a cause of action in negligence against F to recover for his personal injuries

16. Assume that D, while carefully and without negligence, engaged in blasting on his premises, caused damage to P's adjacent building. The damage was solely the result of concussive force.
What is D's liability under these circumstances?
D is

16._____

A. liable to P under a strict liability rule without proof of fault
B. not liable to P unless P can prove negligence
C. liable to P only if rocks or debris thrown by D's blasting damaged P's property
D. not liable to P

17. Assume that D has converted a rare book belonging to A, and is still in possession of the book after A has demanded its return.
If A brings an action in conversion for damages, A is entitled to the

17._____

A. amount he paid for the book
B. market value of the book at the time of conversion
C. market value of the book at the time of judgment, if that is higher than the market value at the time of conversion
D. appraisal value of the book at the time of purchase

18. A owed C $500. B, who told A he needed $500 for a few days, obtained that sum from A and promised to pay C the $500 the following week. B did not pay C, and C instituted an action against B for the money.
Assuming that the necessary proof is preferred, what are the prospects for C's recovery in this case?

18._____

A. C cannot recover because there is no privity between C and B.
B. C may recover as a third party beneficiary of the contract between A and B.
C. C cannot recover because no consideration moved from C to B.
D. C may recover on the theory that B is a constructive trustee of the funds and the Court will impress such a trust to prevent unjust enrichment.

19. P checked a parcel in a public check room at a railroad station and was given a stub with large red identifying numbers on it. In small print at the bottom of the check stub there was the legend: *This contract is made upon the following conditions: The charge is 50¢ a day or fraction thereof for each parcel checked. No claim shall be made in excess of $25.00 for loss or damage to any one parcel.* The parcel was lost through the negligence of the management. The parcel contained fur pieces valued at $5,000. P sues the check room operator for $5,000.
In such a case, P may recover

19._____

A. only $25 because he is bound by the notice on the check stub on the limitation of liability
B. only $25 because by accepting the baggage check he accepted all the contractual provisions thereon

C. $5,000 because he did not have reasonable notice of the terms of the contract and, therefore, could not be deemed to have accepted them
D. $5,000 because no one who invites the public to do business may limit his liability where a loss occurs through negligence.

20. In charging a jury on the issue of damages where there has been a default by a builder in a construction contract which one of the following is NOT a correct charge? 20.____

A. Where there is a substantial defect in the construction, generally the measure of damages is the cost of replacement or repair to conform to the contract.
B. If the breach was unsubstantial and unintentional, the measure of damages is the contract price because the contract has not been performed.
C. If replacement costs to correct the breach are major and are out of proportion to the good to be attained, the measure of damages is the difference in value between the building as contracted for and its value as built.
D. Where a builder pleads substantial performance, the burden of proving the reason for the deviation from the contract and the proper deduction for such difference is on the builder.

KEY (CORRECT ANSWERS)

1.	C	6.	B	11.	B	16.	A
2.	B	7.	C	12.	D	17.	C
3.	A	8.	B	13.	C	18.	B
4.	D	9.	A	14.	B	19.	C
5.	D	10.	A	15.	D	20.	B

EXAMINATION SECTION
TEST 1

DIRECTIONS: Each question or incomplete statement is followed by several suggested answers or completions. Select the one that BEST answers the question or completes the statement. *PRINT THE LETTER OF THE CORRECT ANSWER IN THE SPACE AT THE RIGHT.*

1. P and D signed a contract for the proposed sale of Blackacre. The contract included a description of the property, the selling price, the amount of the purchase money mortgage, and the identity of the parties. It further provided that terms for the payment of principal and interest would be mutually agreed upon at the time the formal contract was concluded. Subsequently, D prepared a contract which provided a schedule of amortization which P found unsatisfactory. P prepared another contract with a somewhat different schedule which he signed and forwarded to D.
D refused to sign and refused to go forward with the sale. P brings an action in specific performance.
In such a case, specific performance should be

   A. *denied* because a material element of the contract is left for future negotiations
   B. *denied* because the terms of the mortgage payments had been omitted; the absence of any element in a contract for the sale of real property vitiates the contract under the Statute of Frauds
   C. *granted* because the defendant cannot take advantage of the failure of a condition precedent where he himself has prevented the condition from being met
   D. *granted* because the contract meets the requirements of the Statute of Frauds, the buyer and seller, the property and the price all being identified

2. Which one of the following statements concerning consideration as an element in contracts is NOT accurate?

   A. Consideration may be defined as a bargained-for exchange.
   B. A promise to make a gift is unenforceable.
   C. An exclusive dealing agreement is not without consideration because the party who gets the exclusive right makes no promise in return; the law implies a duty to use his best efforts.
   D. An agreement which permits one of the parties to terminate at will is enforceable against the other party who did not retain such a right.

3. P entered into a written contract with D which provided that if P could obtain a dealership for D from X, P would receive $10,000 and a percentage of the profits.
P did obtain the dealership for D by bribing X's manager. D knew nothing of this. Subsequently, he does not pay P, and P brings an accounting action against D.
In such a case, P

   A. *can* recover because the contract is valid on its face and the illegal acts committed were not part of that agreement
   B. *cannot* recover because an agent may not recover from his principal compensation for obtaining a contract by illegal means not authorized by the principal
   C. *can* recover because D cannot assert as a defense a wrong committed against X
   D. *cannot* recover because of his illegal conduct but D cannot benefit thereby; D must hold the profits and the $10,000 as a constructive trustee for the benefit of X

4. P, who had a government contract for radar sets, entered into a contract with D for gears needed to construct the sets. Subsequently, P obtained an additional contract for such sets from the Government and advertised for bids for the gears he would need for the second contract. D notified P that unless he gave him the contract for the additional gears and agreed to pay him a higher price on all gears furnished, including the ones needed for the first contract, he would refuse to supply him with any gears at all. Because of the liquidated damage and default clauses in P's contract with the Government and his inability to get enough gears to meet his commitments on the first contract if D breached, P agreed to D's demands and entered into a new contract for all the gears at a higher price. Subsequently, P sued D to recover payments made for goods delivered
In such a case, P

   A. *should succeed* because the contract was voidable on the grounds of duress
   B. *should lose* because, although he was subject to economic duress, the duress that avoids a contract is physical duress or fear of physical duress
   C. *should lose* because there was a recission of the first contract and a valid new contract
   D. *should succeed* partially because there was no consideration for the new price charged for the gears; P should recover the difference between the old contract price and the new contract price for the gears furnished for the first contract

5. Which one of the following is NOT a proper rule of damages for breach of a contract of sale of merchandise to be resold by a purchaser?

   A. The general rule is that the buyer who has contracted to resell goods to a customer is entitled to the difference between the market price on the date of the breach and the price he must pay for cover. In anticipatory breach, he may select either the contract date or the date he was notified that the seller would not perform.
   B. If there are special circumstances made known to the seller at the time the contract was made that put him on notice that his failure to deliver would cause the buyer to breach a contract with his customer, and in fact that second contract is breached, the measure of damages is the damages paid by the buyer to his customer and expenses incurred to satisfy the buyer's breach to this customer.
   C. If the breach is not substantial, the measure of damages is the difference between the value of full performance and the value of the performance that was proffered, or the cost of replacing the non-conforming goods, whichever is more; no buyer has a right to reject goods which substantially conform to the contract.
   D. Mere knowledge by seller that buyer is purchasing for resale is not deemed notice of special circumstances that would entitle the buyer to recover consequential damages.

6. When researching a legal problem, the main objective is to locate primary (mandatory) authority within your jurisdiction.
Primary authority would NOT include

   A. legislation
   B. judicial decisions
   C. administrative rules
   D. law revision commission reports

7. Assume that you are given the name of a case and the citation to either the official reports or unofficial reporter in which it is published.
   The one of the following you should consult in order to obtain the parallel citation is

   A. the state Jurisprudence
   B. Shepard Case Citators
   C. the state Consolidated Laws Service
   D. Corpus Juris Secundum

8. Absent primary (mandatory) authority within this state relating to a legal question under consideration, you would consider persuasive (secondary) authority. Persuasive authority would NOT include

   A. other-state judicial decisions
   B. opinions of legal experts
   C. legislation of another state
   D. obiter dictum in reporter opinions

9. Where there has been no judicial interpretation relevant to a particular legal issue, what source other than the statute itself would you consult in order to determine the existence of documentation which might indicate the legislative intent of a statute enacted by the legislature of the state?

   A. American Jurisprudence 2nd
   B. Manual for the use of the Legislature of the State
   C. McKinney's Session Laws
   D. Abbott's Digest

10. Shepard Case Citators enable you to determine whether the cited case

    A. has been affirmed, reversed, or modified on appeal to a higher tribunal
    B. has been subsequently modified by a statute
    C. is discussed in Corpus Juris Secundum
    D. is listed in the Annotations in McKinney's Consolidated Laws

11. The Shepard Citator unit for Statutes does NOT permit you to shepardize

    A. opinions of the Attorney General of the United States
    B. United States Code
    C. United States treaties
    D. Unconsolidated Laws (McKinney)

12. Assume that you commence your research by using Abbott's Digest and find no cases under the Topic and Key Number assigned to your point of law.
    In this situation, by using the same Topic and Key Number, you can extend your search to all of the following EXCEPT

    A. the Atlantic Digest
    B. the American Digest System
    C. Modern Federal Practice Digest
    D. American Law Reports 2d Digest

13. Rules promulgated by the Courts of the State are published in all of the following publications EXCEPT

    A. State Official Compilation of Codes, Rules, and Regulations
    B. Abbott's Digest
    C. New York Law Journal
    D. McKinney's Consolidated Laws

14. Which of the following is the official report in which cases decided by the New York Court of Appeals are published?

    A. Northeastern Reporter 2d
    B. New York Supplement 2d
    C. New York Reports 2d
    D. Miscellaneous Reports 2d

15. In tracing federal legislative history, all of the following should be considered in order to assist in determining the intent of Congress EXCEPT

    A. Congressional debates
    B. U.S. Government Manual, 1973-1974
    C. Congressional Committee published reports
    D. Congressional Committee published hearings

16. According to the Uniform System of Citations, 11th ed., which one of the following examples would be the proper method of citing the case of Courtney v. Kelmus, decided in the Supreme Court, State of New York, on December 1, 1944, and reported in volume 50 of the New York Supplement 2d on page 897 and in volume 182 of the Miscellaneous Reports on page 498?

    A. 182 Misc. 498, 50 N.Y.S.2d 897
    B. 50 N.Y.S.2d 897, 182 Misc. 498 (Sup. Ct. 1944)
    C. 182 Misc. 498 (Sup. Ct. 1944)
    D. 182 Misc. 498, 50 N.Y.S.2d 897 (Sup. Ct. 1944)

Questions 17-25.

DIRECTIONS: Questions 17 through 25 are to be answered SOLELY on the basis of case law and statutory law in the State.

17. What jurisdiction does the State acquire when a foreign corporation is *doing business* in this state?
    The State

    A. acquires personal jurisdiction over the foreign corporation for any cause of action, no matter where the events which gave rise to it occurred
    B. acquires jurisdiction over only those acts committed by the foreign corporation in the State
    C. always acquires jurisdiction over all of the foreign corporation's foreign subsidiaries
    D. acquires no jurisdiction unless the foreign corporation's property can be attached

18. A defendant does NOT appear in an action when he 18._____
    A. makes a motion which has the effect of extending the time to answer
    B. serves a timely answer
    C. demands a complaint if one is not served with the summons in an action of the Supreme Court
    D. serves a timely notice of appearance

19. With respect to the granting of an order of attachment, it would be CORRECT to state that such an order 19._____
    A. may be granted in a matrimonial action
    B. must be granted where defendant is not a resident or domiciliary of the state and plaintiff would be entitled to a money judgment
    C. is never granted against a New York domiciliary
    D. may be granted where defendant is not a resident or domiciliary of the state and plaintiff would be entitled to a money judgment

20. Which of the following is NOT the function of a bill of particulars? To 20._____
    A. amplify the pleadings
    B. obtain your adversary's evidence
    C. limit proof at trial
    D. prevent surprise at trial

21. Which of the following statements concerning a motion for summary judgement is NOT correct? 21._____
    A. Without a formal cross-motion, the court cannot grant summary judgment to a non-moving party.
    B. The motion shall be granted if the cause of action is established sufficiently to warrant the court as a matter of law in directing judgment.
    C. The motion shall be denied if there is a genuine factual issue requiring a trial.
    D. An affidavit by an attorney without personal knowledge of the facts is of no probative value.

22. Plaintiff may NOT conduct an examination before trial 22._____
    A. of a third-party defendant
    B. of a defendant unless plaintiff first obtains a court order
    C. of a non-party witness unless there are special circumstances shown
    D. unless a note of issue and statement of readiness have been filed

23. In a medical malpractice action based on defendant's alleged negligence in leaving a surgical clamp inside plaintiff, the statute of limitations 23._____
    A. begins to run from the date of the operation
    B. may be extended by the court upon a showing of good cause
    C. need not be pleaded as an affirmative defense
    D. will not begin to run until plaintiff could reasonably have discovered the malpractice

24. When jurisdiction is acquired over a defendant solely on the basis of the *Long-arm* statute (CPLR 302), it would be CORRECT to state that

    A. New York has jurisdiction over every tortious act committed by the defendant outside New York causing injury to property within New York
    B. New York has jurisdiction over a cause of action against a New Jersey domiciliary who drives into New York and runs over plaintiff
    C. defendant's appearance in New York gives the court jurisdiction over causes of action not arising from acts enumerated in the statute
    D. defendant's ownership of real property in New York gives the court jurisdiction over every tortious act committed by him outside New York

25. Where plaintiff joins a claim that is not triable by jury with a claim that is triable by jury as of right, the plaintiff

    A. is entitled to a trial by jury on both claims of action
    B. has split his cause of action
    C. has waived his right to a jury trial on both claims where the claims are based on the same transactions and wrongs
    D. is entitled to a trial by jury only on the claim triable by jury as of right

---

KEY (CORRECT ANSWERS)

1. A		11. A	
2. D		12. D	
3. B		13. B	
4. A		14. C	
5. C		15. D	
6. D		16. D	
7. B		17. A	
8. C		18. C	
9. C		19. D	
10. A		20. B	

21. A
22. C
23. D
24. B
25. C

EXAMINATION SECTION
TEST 1

DIRECTIONS: Each question or incomplete statement is followed by several suggested answers or completions. Select the one that BEST answers the question or completes the statement. *PRINT THE LETTER OF THE CORRECT ANSWER IN THE SPACE AT THE RIGHT.*

1. In payment for a television set, C gave D a $400 note dated January 15, and payable in 30 days. D discounted the note at the S Bank.
   On the date of maturity, C may legally refuse to pay the note if

   A. D used duress in obtaining C's signature
   B. D misrepresented the merchandise he sold to C
   C. C was an infant
   D. D took the completed note from C's desk without C's permission

   1._____

2. A, a general partner in the firm of A and B, died. He left a will leaving all his business and personal property to his wife.
   His wife should then be

   A. legally entitled to become a general partner of the firm immediately
   B. entitled to her husband's share of the firm's net worth
   C. required to carry out, personally or otherwise, the partnership duties formerly carried out by her husband
   D. expected to serve as a general partner until the end of the firm's fiscal year

   2._____

3. A television set was sold to E by the G Appliance Co. for $250 terms 30 days.
   Title to the television set passed to E when

   A. the sale was made
   B. the set was delivered
   C. the set was paid for
   D. 30 days have passed

   3._____

4. A fire insurance contract becomes effective when the

   A. insurance company issues the policy
   B. insured receives the policy
   C. insured pays his first premium
   D. agent agrees to insure the property

   4._____

5. I bought a radio on the installment plan from the H Appliance Co. After the set had been delivered to I, but before he had fully paid for it, vandals broke into I's apartment and stole the radio.
   The loss would be borne by

   A. H Appliance Co.
   B. I
   C. I – only to the extent of what he had already paid
   D. H Appliance Co. and I equally

   5._____

41

6. K sold $500 merchandise to J, terms n/30. K immediately assigned his $500 claim against J to L. After the assignment was made, J returned $100 defective merchandise to K.
   L can collect

   A. $500 from J. J must settle with K.
   B. $500 from K. J must settle with K.
   C. $400 from J and $100 from K.
   D. $500 from J after J has settled with K.

7. A refusal by a creditor to accept a debtor's offer to pay cash in settlement of his debt

   A. discharges the debt
   B. excuses the debtor from interest payments
   C. renews the debt for six years
   D. bars legal action by the creditor on the debt

8. S, the buyer for the dress department of F Stores, was instructed by R, the proprietor, to pay for all merchandise with sixty-day notes. S signed one note given in full payment of a bill of goods, F Stores, by S, Agent; a second was signed, S, Agent for F Stores; and a third was signed, S, Agent.
   The principal could be held liable on

   A. all the notes
   B. none of the notes
   C. the first note only
   D. the first and second notes only

9. M asked B, his bookkeeper, to purchase a fan for the office for not more than $40. B bought a fan for $24 as well as a desk lamp for $16 from the Q Appliance Company.
   The Q Appliance Company legally can collect

   A. $24 from M and $16 from B
   B. $40 from M and compel him to take the lamp
   C. $24 from M and accept the return of the lamp
   D. $40 from M and ask M to collect $16 from B

10. D and F were partners engaged in the wholesale grocery business. Without the knowledge or consent of his partner, D executed and delivered to M a promissory note in payment of a partnership debt. He signed the firm's name on the note.
    On the promissory note, M can legally hold

    A. D only
    B. D and F
    C. neither D nor F
    D. D to the extent of his investment, and F for the balance, if any

11. W, in order to meet the claims of his creditors, borrowed $2500 from P. In order to protect his interest, P insured W's life for $2500. Later, W paid $1500 to P, on account. P continued paying the premiums on W's life insurance policy.
    On W's death, P could collect _____ from the insurance company and $1000 from P's estate.

    A. nothing   B. $1000   C. $1500   D. $2500

12. A principal will ordinarily be held liable for the acts of his agent *only* of these acts are   12.____

    A. to the principal's advantage
    B. to the agent's advantage
    C. within the principal's express instructions
    D. within the actual or apparent scope of the agent's authority

13. A dealer sold and delivered a record player to F. Later, discovering that F was a minor,   13.____
    the dealer sought to avoid the contract and recover the record player.
    Which statement BEST explains why the dealer cannot recover the record player?

    A. Ordinarily a contract between an adult and an infant is voidable at the option of the infant
    B. Infancy is an absolute defense good against all parties
    C. The dealer should have determined F's age before entering into this agreement
    D. An infant is bound only on his contracts for necessaries

14. K, a holder in due course, failed to make proper presentment of a negotiable instrument   14.____
    on the due date. K's failure to present the paper to the party primarily liable, discharged

    A. the maker only
    B. both the maker and the indorsers
    C. all indorsers
    D. K's immediate indorser only

15. If an ultra vires contract has been fully performed by both parties,   15.____

    A. neither party can rescind the contract
    B. the stockholders of the corporation may compel the Board of Directors to rescind the contract
    C. the Board of Directors may rescind the contract without a stockholder's vote
    D. only the other party (not the corporation) may rescind the contract

KEY (CORRECT ANSWERS)

1.	C		6.	C
2.	B		7.	B
3.	A		8.	C
4.	D		9.	A
5.	B		10.	B

11. D
12. D
13. A
14. C
15. A

TEST 2

DIRECTIONS: Each question or incomplete statement is followed by several suggested answers or completions. Select the one that BEST answers the question or completes the statement. *PRINT THE LETTER OF THE CORRECT ANSWER IN THE SPACE AT THE RIGHT.*

1. In a C.O.D. sale, title

    A. passes at the date of the sale
    B. is retained by the seller until delivered to the buyer
    C. passes when the goods are delivered to the carrier
    D. passes when the purchaser receives and pays for the item

    1.____

2. A, and insane person, before so officially adjudged, entered into a contract with B. This contract is

    A. an aleatory contract
    B. voidable at option of A
    C. void
    D. voidable at option of B

    2.____

3. A bill of lading serves four distinct functions as
    I. a receipt
    II. a contract
    III. evidence of the kind, quality, and the quantity of good shipped, *and*
    IV. ....

    A. an invoice
    B. evidence of liability
    C. evidence of title
    D. a purchase order

    3.____

4. Liquidated damages

    A. constitute compensation which parties have agreed upon to be paid which will follow a breach of contract
    B. are damages which result from particular circumstances in a case
    C. are damages resulting when a wrong is established but no real damage is shown, or proven
    D. are synonymous with *mitigated damages*

    4.____

5. An executory contract is

    A. an implied contract
    B. a contract used in wills
    C. one fully performed
    D. one not yet performed

    5.____

6. Champerty is

    A. encouragement of liquidation by contract
    B. an unlicensed transaction
    C. in restraint of trade
    D. a form of price-fixing

    6.____

7. Contracts made on Sundays and legal holidays, including checks and promissory notes, not consummated or calling for performance on such days, are

    A. void
    B. voidable
    C. valid
    D. contrary to public policy

    7.____

2 (#2)

8. The substitution of a new contract, or a new debtor, for an existing one, is called 8._____

   A. a *condition precedent* B. a *quasi contract*
   C. unenforceable D. a *novation*

9. The right of *stoppage-in-transitu* arises only when an unpaid seller has 9._____

   A. made a mistake in price
   B. defaulted in paying creditors
   C. shipped goods to a buyer who is insolvent
   D. admitted a fourth partner

10. Design patents are good for _____ years. 10._____

    A. 7 B. 17 C. 28 D. no time limit

11. When a seller has a voidable title to goods because of fraud, a *bona fide* purchaser for value acquires _____ title. 11._____

    A. voidable B. valid C. defective D. no

12. In this state, a contract for the sale of goods comes under the Statute of Frauds if the value is _____ or upward. 12._____

    A. $50 B. $200 C. $250 D. $500

13. An insurance company receives its right to seek payment from a third party who was negligent and caused the loss from the _____ clause. 13._____

    A. subrogation B. contributions
    C. co-insurance D. general average

14. An addition to a will is known as a(n) 14._____

    A. amendment B. allonge
    C. continuance D. codicil

15. On July 14, W in New York, shipped goods to C, in Rochester. The goods were sent *F.O.B. Rochester* as directed in the written order of July 8. The goods arrived at the station in Rochester on July 18 and C was notified. On July 21, C picked up the goods at the station. 15._____
    The title to the goods passed to C on July _____ .

    A. 18 B. 8 C. 21 D. 14

KEY (CORRECT ANSWERS)

1. C
2. B
3. C
4. A
5. D

6. A
7. C
8. D
9. D
10. A

11. B
12. D
13. A
14. D
15. A

EXAMINATION SECTION

Case 1

DIRECTIONS FOR THIS SECTION:
   Each of the law cases described is followed by several legal principles. These principles may be either real or imaginary, but for purposes of this test you are to assume them to be valid. Following each legal principle are four statements regarding the possible applicability or inapplicability of the principle to the law case. You are to select the ONE statement which most appropriately describes the applicability or inapplicability of the principle to the law case. *PRINT THE LETTER OF THE CORRECT ANSWER IN THE SPACE AT THE RIGHT.*

These questions do not presuppose any specific legal knowledge on your part; you are to arrive at your answers entirely by the ordinary processes of logical reasoning.

CASE 1

Questions 1-4.

   Mr. A, a fireman, tripped on a defective step, fell down a flight of stairs, and was injured while fighting a fire in Mr. B's house. Although it was a cold day, Mr. B had not turned on the heat in his tenants' apartments, which was a violation of state law. Mr. A sues Mr. B for his injuries.

1. By statute, a landlord's failure to heat his tenants' apartments on a cold day is an offense punishable by fine.
   The above principle is
   A. *applicable* since his tenants are entitled to heat from Mr. B on a cold day
   B. *applicable* since Mr. B violated the law in failing to heat his tenants' apartments
   C. *inapplicable* since Mr. A is seeking damages from Mr. B, and Mr. B is not being prosecuted for failure to heat his tenants' apartments
   D. *inapplicable* since Mr. B could not foresee that a fire would break out in his house

   1._____

2. By statute, the owner of a building is absolutely liable to a fireman injured as a result of the owner's violation of a state law.
   The above principle is
   A. *applicable* since Mr. A was injured while fighting a fire in Mr. B's house
   B. *applicable* since Mr. B's failure to heat his tenants' apartments was a violation of state law
   C. *inapplicable* since Mr. B's failure to heat his tenants' apartments did not contribute to Mr. A's injuries
   D. *inapplicable* since Mr. B could not foresee that a fire would break out in his house

   2._____

3. The owner of a building owes a duty to firemen who may enter the building to fight a fire to keep the premises in a reasonably safe condition.
   The above principle is
   A. *applicable* since Mr. B's failure to heat his tenants' apartments was a violation of state law
   B. *applicable* since the defective step was a hazard against which it was Mr. B's duty to protect Mr. A

   3._____

C. *inapplicable* since Mr. B could not foresee that a fire would break out in his building
D. *inapplicable* since Mr. B could not know that Mr. A would be among the firemen who fought the fire in his building

4. One who negligently starts a fire is liable to a fireman injured while fighting the fire. The above principle is
   A. *applicable* since Mr. A was injured while fighting a fire in Mr. B's building
   B. *applicable* since all persons are under a duty not to start fires negligently
   C. *inapplicable* since Mr. A should have seen the defective step before tripping on it
   D. *inapplicable* since there is nothing to indicate that the fire started as a result of Mr. B's negligence

4._____

CASE 2

Questions 5-9.

Mr. A is prosecuted for murdering Mr. B. Mr. A does not deny killing Mr. B, but claims (1) that he killed Mr. B in self-defense; (2) that he was insane at the time he killed Mr. B; and (3) that Mr. C, who was standing nearby at the time of the killing, had threatened to kill Mr. A if Mr. A did not kill Mr. B. Mr. A is telling the truth.

5. By statute, one who plans, counsels, abets, assists in, or encourages a murder is guilty of murder.
   The above principle is
   A. *applicable* since Mr. C encouraged and abetted the murder of Mr. B
   B. *applicable* since Mr. A was insane at the time of the killing of Mr. B
   C. *inapplicable* since Mr. C is not being prosecuted for murder
   D. *inapplicable* since Mr. A, not Mr. C, killed Mr. B

5._____

6. One who is compelled by fear of bodily harm to himself to commit what would otherwise be a crime is not guilty of the crime.
   The above principle is
   A. *applicable* since Mr. A was insane at the time he killed Mr. B
   B. *applicable* since Mr. C compelled Mr. A to kill Mr. B
   C. *inapplicable* since Mr. C himself did not kill Mr. B
   D. *inapplicable* since anyone can claim that someone else compelled him to commit a crime he committed

6._____

7. Insanity is not a defense in a prosecution for murder unless it resulted in the accused's failure to know the nature of his act and to know that it was wrong.
   The above principle is
   A. *applicable* since Mr. A was insane at the time he killed Mr. B
   B. *applicable* since Mr. A must have known the nature of his act and known that it was wrong, or Mr. C would not have had to threaten him to make him kill Mr. B
   C. *inapplicable* since people should not be permitted to get away with murder simply by claiming insanity
   D. *inapplicable* since Mr. A, not Mr. C, is being prosecuted for murder

7._____

8. By statute, one who kills in self-defense is not guilty of murder. 8._____
   The above principle is
   A. *applicable* since Mr. A killed Mr. B in self-defense
   B. *applicable* since Mr. A was insane at the time he killed Mr. B
   C. *inapplicable* since Mr. A, not Mr. C, is being prosecuted for murder
   D. *inapplicable* since anyone can claim self-defense to avoid a prosecution for murder

9. By statute, the penalty for murder in the first degree is death, unless the jury 9._____
   recommends life imprisonment.
   The above principle is
   A. *applicable* since Mr. A is being prosecuted for murder
   B. *applicable* since a crime as serious as murder requires the imposition of harsh penalties
   C. *inapplicable* since Mr. A, not Mr. C, is being prosecuted for murder
   D. *inapplicable* since Mr. A, who killed Mr. B in self-defense and under compulsion, is not guilty of murder

CASE 3

Questions 10-14.

Mr. A was prosecuted for robbery in hitting Mr. B on the head with a hammer and taking Mr. B's watch, worth $75.00. Mr. A was acquitted. Mr. A now seeks to avoid a new prosecution for the crime of larceny in stealing Mr. B's wallet. Mr. A seeks to avoid the second prosecution.

10. The crime of robbery is made up of two other crimes, assault and larceny. 10._____
    The above principle is
    A. *applicable* since Mr. A was originally accused of robbery
    B. *applicable* since Mr. B's original prosecution for robbery was necessarily also a prosecution for larceny, and he cannot be tried again for the same crime
    C. *inapplicable* since Mr. A was not originally prosecuted for larceny
    D. *inapplicable* since Mr. A is not now being charged with assault

11. A person convicted of a crime based on a particular act cannot again be 11._____
    prosecuted for the same crime based upon the same act.
    The above principle is
    A. *applicable* since Mr. A was originally charged with larceny and assault and is now being charged with larceny based upon the same act
    B. *applicable* since the same larceny is involved in this prosecution as was involved in the original prosecution
    C. *inapplicable* since Mr. A was acquitted on the original prosecution
    D. *inapplicable* since Mr. A has not yet been convicted in the second prosecution

12. A person acquitted of a crime based on a particular act cannot again be 12._____
    prosecuted for any crime based upon the same act.
    The above principle is
    A. *applicable* since Mr. A is now being prosecuted for a crime based upon the same act of a crime upon which he was acquitted
    B. *applicable* since the original prosecution was for robbery

C. *inapplicable* since Mr. A has not yet been convicted in the second prosecution
D. *inapplicable* since this is a criminal prosecution and not a suit for damages

13. By statute, a person found guilty of petty larceny may be sentenced to not more than two years in a state penitentiary.
    The above principle is
    A. *applicable* since Mr. A is being prosecuted for petty larceny as Mr. B's watch was worth less than $100.00
    B. *applicable* since petty larceny is a less serious crime than grand larceny and deserves a lighter penalty
    C. *inapplicable* since Mr. A's original prosecution was for robbery
    D. *inapplicable* since Mr. A cannot be re-tried for larceny and, therefore, cannot be found guilty

14. The prosecution cannot appeal to a higher court from the acquittal of an accused in a criminal trial.
    The above principle is
    A. *applicable* since Mr. A was acquitted in the original prosecution
    B. *applicable* since such an appeal would violate the prohibition against double jeopardy
    C. *inapplicable* since Mr. A is now being prosecuted for larceny
    D. *inapplicable* since the prosecution has not sought to appeal Mr. A's acquittal to a higher court

CASE 4

Questions 15-21.

Mr. D, a printer, prints a thousand copies of a leaflet demanding that all Jews be expelled from the United States and that all Blacks be sterilized, and charging certain prominent Jews and Blacks with a variety of crimes they, in fact, did not commit. Before he can distribute the leaflets, Mr. D is arrested by the local police and charged with criminal libel, and his leaflets are confiscated. Mr. D is also called before a committee of the United States House of Representatives, where he refuses, on the ground of self-incrimination, to answer questions about the leaflets. He is cited by the Committee for contempt for failure to answer the questions.

15. One who is falsely charged with a crime may sue his accuser for damages for libel or slander.
    The above principle is
    A. *applicable* since Mr. D charged prominent Jews and Blacks with crimes they had not committed
    B. *applicable* since Mr. D knew that the charges relating to crimes were false
    C. *inapplicable* since Mr. D printed only a small number of leaflets
    D. *inapplicable* since Mr. D is not being sued for libel or slander by the prominent Jews or Blacks

Case 4

16. A libel or slander is perpetrated only when it is communicated to another person by the deliberate act of the perpetrator.
    The above principle is
    A. *applicable* since the local police must have read the defamatory leaflet
    B. *applicable* since Mr. D never had the chance to communicate the libels or slanders to other persons by his deliberate act
    C. *inapplicable* since Mr. D must have thought that the prominent Jews and Blacks had committed the crimes he charged
    D. *inapplicable* since Mr. D has the constitutional right of freedom of speech

    16._____

17. Printed matter may not be censored until after its distribution is begun.
    The above principle is
    A. *applicable* since Mr. D's leaflets were confiscated before they could be distributed
    B. *applicable* since Mr. D is not being sued for libel
    C. *inapplicable* since Mr. D's leaflets were vicious and defamatory
    D. *inapplicable* since the local police were acting in the public interest in keeping vicious and defamatory literature from being circulated

    17._____

18. The First Amendment to the United States Constitution and State Constitutions guarantee to all persons freedom of speech and freedom of the press.
    The above principle is
    A. *applicable* since Mr. D must have believed that what he printed was true
    B. *applicable* since Mr. D was prevented by the local police from exercising his freedom of speech and freedom of the press by their arresting him and confiscating his leaflets
    C. *inapplicable* since no one should have the right or the freedom to tell lies about others
    D. *inapplicable* since Mr. D had not distributed any of the leaflets at the time of his arrest

    18._____

19. The Fifth Amendment to the United States Constitution protects all persons from being forced to incriminate themselves.
    The above principle is
    A. *applicable* since Mr. D was asked questions about the leaflets by the Committee at the same time that he was being charged with criminal libel with regard to the same leaflets
    B. *applicable* since the leaflets were false and defamatory
    C. *inapplicable* since the Constitution should not be used as a shield to protect vicious criminals
    D. *inapplicable* since the prominent Jews and Blacks are not suing Mr. D for libel or slander

    19._____

20. A person who justifiably claims the privilege against self-incrimination may not be cited for contempt by a Congressional Committee.
    The above principle is
    A. *applicable* since Mr. D's leaflets were confiscated by the local police
    B. *applicable* since Mr. D was justified in believing that answers to the Committee's questions would assist his prosecution for criminal libel
    C. *inapplicable* since it is in the public interest that Congress not be denied information about activities such as these
    D. *inapplicable* since vicious and criminal defamers like Mr. D should not go unpunished

    20._____

21. Ethnic groups, such as Blacks and Jews, cannot themselves sue for libel or slander of the groups.
    The above principle is
    A. *applicable* since such groups are too large to be represented in court
    B. *applicable* since the damages that would have to be paid after a judgment would be too large
    C. *inapplicable* since Mr. D must have believed his charges to be true
    D. *inapplicable* since Jewish and Black groups are not suing Mr. D for libel or slander

21._____

CASE 5

Questions 22-24.

Mr. A, a resident of the city of Atlanta, Georgia, brings a suit in Federal Court against the Georgia state legislature, charging that the legislature has failed for many years to reapportion state legislature districts so as to reflect population shifts, as required by the Georgia State Constitution. As a result, Mr. A says, sparsely-populated rural areas have the same representation in the legislature as heavily-populated urban areas.

22. State courts do not ordinarily decide cases concerning political questions in the province of the legislature.
    The above principle is
    A. *applicable* since the apportionment of the legislature is a political question
    B. *applicable* since a State Court cannot apportion legislature districts
    C. *inapplicable* since State Court judges are usually elected by popular vote
    D. *inapplicable* since this suit is in a Federal, not a State, Court

22._____

23. Federal Courts have a duty to enforce provisions of the United States Constitution, and to remedy violations.
    The above principle is
    A. *applicable* since the apportionment of the legislature is manifestly unfair
    B. *applicable* since the United States Constitution guarantees to each state a republican form of government
    C. *inapplicable* since Mr. A is charging a violation of the Georgia Constitution
    D. *inapplicable* since Mr. A is not claiming racial discrimination

23._____

24. The Georgia Constitution guarantees to all citizens of Georgia the equal protection of the law and the equal right to vote.
    The above principle is
    A. *applicable* since Mr. A is not claiming racial discrimination
    B. *applicable* since, by the apportionment of the Georgia legislature, Mr. A's vote counted for less than did the vote of a voter in rural Georgia
    C. *inapplicable* since Mr. A had the right to vote
    D. *inapplicable* since a Federal Court should not interfere in matters that are exclusively the affairs of sovereign states

24._____

CASE 6

Questions 25-28.

Mr. D, the owner of a movie theatre, exhibited a motion picture therein entitled "Bare Bosoms," which had been licensed by the State for exhibition. In front of the theatre, Mr. D displayed "stills" from the film. Mr. D received a summons from the Police Department charging him with violating a state law by publicly displaying obscene posters. The State licensing law prohibits the licensing authorities from licensing motion pictures which are obscene.

25. By statute, it is a crime to exhibit publicly an obscene motion picture.
 The above principle is
 A. *applicable* since impressionable children must be protected from obscene motion pictures
 B. *applicable* since Mr. D exhibited an obviously obscene motion picture
 C. *inapplicable* since Mr. D is not being charged with exhibiting an obscene motion picture
 D. *inapplicable* since the statute is unconstitutional

25._____

26. The freedom of the press and freedom of speech guaranteed by the First Amendment to the United States Constitution protect motion pictures and excerpts from motion pictures.
 The above principle is
 A. *applicable* since Mr. D would not jeopardize his license to operate a movie theatre by exhibiting an obscene film
 B. *applicable* since the charge against Mr. D involves the display of an excerpt from a motion picture
 C. *inapplicable* since Mr. D is not being charged with exhibiting an obscene motion picture
 D. *inapplicable* since the statute is unconstitutional

26._____

27. The freedom of the press and freedom of speech guaranteed by the First Amendment to the United States Constitution do not protect obscenity.
 The above principle is
 A. *applicable* since the Police Department's objection to the posters is that they are obscene
 B. *applicable* since obscenity impairs the moral standards of the community
 C. *inapplicable* since it is up to parents to protect their children from harmful obscenity
 D. *inapplicable* since the statute is unconstitutional

27._____

28. By statute, the Licensing Commission may license motion pictures for public exhibition only if they are found not to be obscene.
 The above principle is
 A. *applicable* since the State must protect the public from obscenity
 B. *applicable* since, if the Licensing Commission found that the motion picture was not obscene, it necessarily found that excerpts from the motion picture were not obscene
 C. *inapplicable* since the motion picture is clearly obscene
 D. *inapplicable* since it is the duty of parents, not the State, to protect children from obscenity

28._____

CASE 7

Questions 29-34.

Mr. A, a passenger riding on the back platform of a train, falls off the train and down an embankment as the train lurches violently to a stop to avoid hitting a cow standing on the tracks, through no fault of the railroad or the engineer. Mr. B, another passenger, hears Mr. A's cry for help and is injured while attempting to rescue Mr. A. Mr. B sues the railroad company for his injuries.

29. The owner of any animal or bird is liable for injuries resulting from its presence on or within ten feet of a public highway or a railroad right of way.
The above principle is
  A. *applicable* since the presence of the cow on the tracks contributed to Mr. B's injuries
  B. *applicable* since it is an owner's obligation to confine and control his livestock
  C. *inapplicable* since Mr. B's suit is against the railroad, not against the owner of the cow
  D. *inapplicable* since the presence of the cow on the tracks contributed to Mr. A's injuries, not to Mr. B's

29._____

30. It is a criminal offense to stop a railroad train suddenly enough to endanger passengers riding on its platform.
The above principle is
  A. *applicable* since the sudden stop of the train contributed to Mr. B's injuries
  B. *applicable* since the sudden stop of the train contributed to Mr. A's injuries
  C. *inapplicable* since the sudden stop did not contribute to Mr. B's injuries
  D. *inapplicable* since Mr. B's suit is for damages and is not a criminal prosecution

30._____

31. A railroad which negligently imperils a passenger is liable for injuries sustained by those going to his rescue.
The above principle is
  A. *applicable* since Mr. B was injured while attempting to rescue Mr. A
  B. *applicable* since the sudden stop threw Mr. A off the train
  C. *inapplicable* since the sudden stop of the train was not caused by the railroad's negligence
  D. *inapplicable* since the cow's owner could not foresee that it would wander onto the tracks

31._____

32. A railroad must insure its employees against injuries suffered as a result of the operation of its trains.
The above principle is
  A. *applicable* since Mr. B was injured as a result of the operation of a train by the railroad
  B. *applicable* since Mr. A was imperiled as a result of the operation of a train by the railroad
  C. *inapplicable* since there is no indication that the railroad was insured
  D. *inapplicable* since Mr. B was not an employee of the railroad

32._____

33. By statute, a railroad is absolutely liable for injuries caused by the negligence of its employees.
    The above principle is
    A. *applicable* since Mr. A was imperiled while riding on a train operated by an employee of the railroad
    B. *applicable* since Mr. B was injured during a journey on a train operated by an employee of the railroad
    C. *inapplicable* since the railroad's engineer was not negligent in the operation of the train
    D. *inapplicable* since Mr. B, not Mr. A, is suing the railroad for his injuries

    33._____

34. By statute, no passenger is permitted to ride on the platform of a moving railroad train, and a railroad is not liable to a passenger injured while riding on a platform.
    The above principle is
    A. *applicable* since Mr. A was riding on the platform of the train when he was thrown from the train
    B. *applicable* since Mr. A would not have been imperiled had he not been riding on the platform
    C. *inapplicable* since Mr. B, not Mr. A, is suing the railroad for his injuries
    D. *inapplicable* since the engineer was not negligent

    34._____

CASE 8

Questions 35-37.

During the trial of Mr. D for a criminal offense, the judge admonishes the prosecutor for his conduct prejudicial to Mr. D and declares a mistrial before the case can be submitted to the jury. Mr. D now seeks to avoid a second trial on the same charges.

35. Once a jury has been impaneled and a trial has been commenced in a criminal prosecution, the defendant has been placed in jeopardy and cannot be tried again for the same offense.
    The above principle is
    A. *applicable* since the judge should not have declared a mistrial under the circumstances
    B. *applicable* since the original trial had commenced
    C. *inapplicable* since the mistrial was declared for Mr. D's protection
    D. *inapplicable* since the judge would not have declared a mistrial had he known that Mr. D could not be tried again

    35._____

36. A trial judge may be censured by the governor of the state in which he sits for improperly declaring a mistrial.
    The above principle is
    A. *applicable* since the judge improperly declared a mistrial
    B. *applicable* since the proper administration of justice requires that judges not declare mistrials without compelling necessity
    C. *inapplicable* since the mistrial was declared for Mr. D's protection
    D. *inapplicable* since Mr. D is seeking to avoid being tried again, not to have the trial judge censured

    36._____

37. Only the death or severe illness of a member of the jury or of someone whose presence is indispensable to the completion of a criminal trial is sufficient ground for a mistrial and a subsequent retrial of a defendant.
The above principle is
A. *applicable* since the judge was not justified in declaring a mistrial under the circumstances
B. *applicable* since the mistrial was not declared as a result of the death or illness of a juror or an indispensable party
C. *inapplicable* since the judge declared a mistrial for the protection of Mr. D
D. *inapplicable* since the judge would not have declared a mistrial had he known Mr. D could not be retried

CASE 9

Questions 38-40.

Mr. A fails to remove the snow from the public sidewalk in front of his home after a snowstorm. Mr. B falls in the snow on the sidewalk and sues Mr. A for his injuries.

38. The condition and safety of public sidewalks are responsibilities of the municipality in which they are located which the municipality cannot delegate to anyone else.
The above principle is
A. *applicable* since the municipality could foresee that Mr. A might fail to clear the sidewalk of snow on which Mr. B fell
B. *applicable* since Mr. A had no responsibility to Mr. B to clear the sidewalk of snow
C. *inapplicable* since Mr. A should have foreseen that a pedestrian might be injured by the accumulation of snow in front of his home
D. *inapplicable* since the municipality could not foresee that Mr. B would be injured by the accumulation of snow in front of Mr. A's home

39. It is an offense, punishable by fine, for a homeowner to fail to clear the snow from the public sidewalk in front of his home within four hours after the end of a snowfall.
The above principle is
A. *applicable* since Mr. B would not have been injured had Mr. A cleared the snow from the public sidewalk in front of his home
B. *applicable* since no municipality has sufficient facilities to clear all public sidewalks within four hours after a snowfall
C. *inapplicable* since Mr. A is suing Mr. B for personal injuries, and no prosecution for an offense is involved
D. *inapplicable* since Mr. A could not foresee that Mr. B would be injured by the accumulation of snow on the sidewalk

40. A homeowner is liable to persons injured on his property, unless they are trespassers.
    The above principle is
    A. *applicable* since Mr. B was not a trespasser
    B. *applicable* since Mr. A should have foreseen that pedestrians like Mr. B might fall on the snow in front of his home
    C. *inapplicable* since it was the municipality's duty to keep the sidewalk in front of Mr. A's home safe for pedestrians
    D. *inapplicable* since Mr. B fell on the public sidewalk, not on Mr. A's property

40._____

CASE 10

Questions 41-43

K Water Company agreed with the City Council of L Town to supply L Town with water for all municipal purposes, including water to be used in the homes of L Town's residents, water for extinguishing fires, water to wash L Town's streets, etc. One week later, L Town's fire department responded promptly to a call from Mr. A, a resident of L Town, and discovered that his home was afire. The fire hydrant near Mr. A's home, however, failed to produce the water needed to extinguish the blaze, and Mr. A's home burned to the ground. Mr. A now sues K Water Company for failing to supply water to extinguish the fire.

41. A municipality owes its residents a duty to be reasonably diligent in extinguishing fires in their homes.
    The above principle is
    A. *applicable* since L Town's fire department did not extinguish the fire in Mr. A's home
    B. *applicable* since K Water Company owed Mr. A the same duty as L Town owed to Mr. A
    C. *inapplicable* since L Town's fire department could not foresee that a fire would consume Mr. A's home so quickly
    D. *inapplicable* since Mr. A is seeking to recover damages from K Water Company for the destruction of his home, not from L Town

41._____

42. Only a direct beneficiary of a contract may sue the party who violates it for damages resulting from the violation, not an incidental beneficiary.
    The above principle is
    A. *applicable* since Mr. A is suing K Water Company, not L Town, for the destruction of his home
    B. *applicable* since the contract was intended to provide L Town with water for all of its municipal functions, and Mr. A, who himself was not a party to the contract, was, like all other residents of L Town, only an incidental beneficiary of the contract
    C. *inapplicable* since K Water Company could not foresee that a fire would break out in Mr. A's home
    D. *inapplicable* since it was L Town's primary duty to protect Mr. A's home from fire damage

42._____

43. By statute, a water company under contract with a municipality to provide it with water for its municipal functions must test and inspect its fire hydrants every three months after installation.
    The above principle is
    A. *applicable* since the fire hydrant near Mr. A's home did not produce the water needed to extinguish the fire in Mr. A's home
    B. *applicable* since K Water Company is a public utility which owes to the public a high degree of care in maintaining its facilities
    C. *inapplicable* since Mr. A was not a party to the contract with K Water Company
    D. *inapplicable* since the fire in Mr. A's home occurred only one week after the execution of the contract

43._____

CASE 11

Questions 44-47.

Mr. D was born in the United States. In January, 1958, he traveled to Cuba and joined Fidel Castro's rebel forces in the mountains. At that time, Castro's men were fighting the army of the Cuban government under President Batista. Later, in 1958, Mr. D returned to the United States. The United States Government now seeks to deport Mr. D on the grounds that he is an alien, since he lost his citizenship by fighting in the army of a foreign country and that he was convicted of the crime of grand larceny in 1946.

44. The commission of the crime of grand larceny by an alien is an act of "moral turpitude" and warrants the deportation of the alien from the United States.
    The above principle is
    A. *applicable* since Mr. D committed the crime of grand larceny
    B. *applicable* since Mr. D is an alien
    C. *inapplicable* since Mr. D was a citizen, and not an alien, at the time he committed the crime of grand larceny
    D. *inapplicable* since Mr. D was already convicted of the crime of grand larceny

44._____

45. Service in the army of a foreign country deprives an American citizen of his citizenship and makes him an alien.
    The above principle is
    A. *applicable* since Mr. D served in Castro's rebel forces
    B. *applicable* since Castro has admitted that he was a Communist at the time he fought the Cuban Army in the mountains
    C. *inapplicable* since Mr. D did not intend to lose his American citizenship
    D. *inapplicable* since Castro's soldiers were rebels in 1958 and were not the army of a foreign country

45._____

46. By statute, no native-born American citizen shall lose his citizenship unless and until he becomes a citizen of another country.
    The above principle is
    A. *applicable* since Mr. D is a native-born American citizen
    B. *applicable* since Mr. D never became a citizen of another country
    C. *inapplicable* since Mr. D returned to the United States in 1958
    D. *inapplicable* since Castro's forces were not the army of a foreign country in 1958

46._____

47. The United States Constitution provides that all persons born in the United States shall be citizens of the United States.
    The above principle is
    A. *applicable* since Mr. D was born in the United States
    B. *applicable* since Mr. D never intended to lose his American citizenship
    C. *inapplicable* since Mr. D fought in Castro's rebel forces
    D. *inapplicable* since American citizens should not join the armed forces of foreign countries

47._____

CASE 12

Questions 48-51

Mr. A, having deposited $1,000.00 in a new checking account, issues a 600.00 check to Mr. B. Unknown to Mr. A, Mr. C had forged Mr. A's name on a $1,000.00 check and had cashed it at Mr. A's bank, leaving no balance in the account. Mr. A's check to Mr. B was returned to Mr. B marked "insufficient funds." The District Attorney now seeks to prosecute Mr. A for larceny for issuing a bad check to Mr. B.

48. By statute, issuing a check on a checking account knowing that there is insufficient money in the account to cover the check, is larceny.
    The above principle is
    A. *applicable* since Mr. A gave the $600.00 check to Mr. B when his checking account had less than $600.00 in it
    B. *applicable* since Mr. C forged Mr. A's name on a check
    C. *inapplicable* since Mr. A did not know that the bank had cashed the forged check which depleted his account
    D. *inapplicable* since there was sufficient money in the account to pay the forged check

48._____

49. A payee of a check which is returned to him marked "insufficient funds" may sue the maker of the check for the amount of the check.
    The above principle is
    A. *applicable* since the $600.00 check was returned to its payee, Mr. B, marked "insufficient funds"
    B. *applicable* since it would be injust to Mr. B if he had no way to recover the amount of the check
    C. *inapplicable* since Mr. A did not know that Mr. C had drawn a forged check on his account
    D. *inapplicable* since this is a criminal prosecution against Mr. A, not a suit for the amount of the check by Mr. B

49._____

50. Forgery is a felony punishable by imprisonment in the State penitentiary.
    The above principle is
    A. *applicable* since Mr. C forged Mr. A's name on a check
    B. *applicable* since Mr. A did not know that Mr. C had signed Mr. A's name on a check
    C. *inapplicable* since Mr. A, not Mr. C, is being prosecuted
    D. *inapplicable* since Mr. B, not Mr. A, lost money as a result of Mr. C's actions

50._____

51. A bank which pays out money on a forged check is liable for the amount of the check to the depositor.
The above principle is
A. *applicable* since the bank paid out Mr. A's money on a forged check
B. *applicable* since a bank owes to its depositors a duty to pay out money only on checks containing their genuine signatures
C. *inapplicable* since the bank did not know that the signature was forged
D. *inapplicable* since Mr. A is being prosecuted and is not making a claim against the bank

51._____

CASE 13

Questions 52-56.

Mr. A lends his new Buick automobile to Mr. B, who has no license to drive. Mr. B, who has little driving experience, carelessly sideswipes Mrs. C. After stopping to assist Mrs. C, Mr. B drives on. The steering wheel of the automobile comes off in Mr. B's hands, and the automobile hits Mr. D, severely injuring him. Mrs. C and Mr. D sue Mr. A, the Buick Company, and their insurance companies for personal injuries.

52. By statute, the owner of an automobile is liable for damages to one injured through the negligence of a person driving the automobile with the owner's permission.
The above principle is
A. *applicable* since Mr. B had no license to drive
B. *applicable* since Mr. B's negligent driving injured Mrs. C, and Mr. B had Mr. A's permission to use the automobile
C. *inapplicable* since the automobile was new
D. *inapplicable* since Mr. A could not foresee that the automobile would strike Mrs. C

52._____

53. The manufacturer of a new automobile is liable to one injured as a result of a defect in its mechanism.
The above principle is
A. *applicable* since Mr. D was injured as a result of a defect in the steering wheel of the automobile
B. *applicable* since Mr. B had Mr. A's permission to drive the automobile
C. *inapplicable* since Mr. B had no license to drive
D. *inapplicable* since the Buick Company could not foresee that Mr. D would be injured as a result of the defect in the steering mechanism

53._____

54. The owner of an automobile is not liable for injuries suffered by its driver unless the latter has a license to drive.
The above principle is
A. *applicable* since Mr. B did not have a license to drive
B. *applicable* since Mr. B was driving the automobile with Mr. A's permission
C. *inapplicable* since Mr. A could not foresee that the steering wheel would come off in Mr. B's hands
D. *inapplicable* since Mr. B is not suing Mr. A for injuries

54._____

Case 13

55. By statute, it is a criminal offense to drive an automobile without a license to drive. The above principle is
    A. *applicable* since Mr. B drove the automobile without having a license to drive
    B. *applicable* since the public must be protected against unlicensed drivers
    C. *inapplicable* since this is a suit for damages by Mrs. C and Mr. D and not a criminal prosecution
    D. *inapplicable* since Mr. A would not have lent Mr. B his automobile had he known Mr. B did not have a license to drive

    55._____

56. By statute, an automobile must be inspected for defects in its mechanism every three years. The above principle is
    A. *applicable* since an inspection would have disclosed the defect in the steering mechanism
    B. *applicable* since Mr. D was injured as a result of a defect in the mechanism of Mr. A's automobile
    C. *inapplicable* since the automobile was new and need not have been inspected
    D. *inapplicable* since Mr. A could not foresee that the steering wheel would come loose while Mr. B was driving the automobile

    56._____

KEYS (CORRECT ANSWERS)

CASE 1
1. C
2. C
3. B
4. D

CASE 2
5. C
6. B
7. B
8. A
9. D

CASE 3
10. B
11. C
12. A
13. D
14. D

CASE 4
15. D
16. B
17. A
18. B
19. A
20. B
21. D

CASE 5
22. D
23. C
24. B

CASE 6
25. C
26. B
27. A
28. B

CASE 7
29. C
30. D
31. C
32. D
33. C
34. C

CASE 8
35. B
36. D
37. B

CASE 9
38. B
39. C
40. D

CASE 10
41. D
42. B
43. D

CASE 11
44. C
45. D
46. B
47. A

CASE 12
48. C
49. D
50. C
51. D

CASE 13
52. B
53. A
54. D
55. C
56. C

PREPARING WRITTEN MATERIAL

PARAGRAPH REARRANGEMENT
COMMENTARY

The sentences which follow are in scrambled order. You are to rearrange them in proper order and indicate the letter choice containing the correct answer at the space at the right.

Each group of sentences in this section is actually a paragraph presented in scrambled order. Each sentence in the group has a place in that paragraph; no sentence is to be left out. You are to read each group of sentences and decide upon the best order in which to put the sentences so as to form as well-organized paragraph.

The questions in this section measure the ability to solve a problem when all the facts relevant to its solution are not given.

More specifically, certain positions of responsibility and authority require the employee to discover connections between events sometimes, apparently, unrelated. In order to do this, the employee will find it necessary to correctly infer that unspecified events have probably occurred or are likely to occur. This ability becomes especially important when action must be taken on incomplete information.

Accordingly, these questions require competitors to choose among several suggested alternatives, each of which presents a different sequential arrangement of the events. Competitors must choose the MOST logical of the suggested sequences.

In order to do so, they may be required to draw on general knowledge to infer missing concepts or events that are essential to sequencing the given events. Competitors should be careful to infer only what is essential to the sequence. The plausibility of the wrong alternatives will always require the inclusion of unlikely events or of additional chains of events which are NOT essential to sequencing the given events.

It's very important to remember that you are looking for the best of the four possible choices, and that the best choice of all may not even be one of the answers you're given to choose from.

There is no one right way to solve these problems. Many people have found it helpful to first write out the order of the sentences, as they would have arranged them, on their scrap paper before looking at the possible answers. If their optimum answer is there, this can save them some time. If it isn't, this method can still give insight into solving the problem. Others find it most helpful to just go through each of the possible choices, contrasting each as they go along. You should use whatever method feels comfortable, and works, for you.

While most of these types of questions are not that difficult, we've added a higher percentage of the difficult type, just to give you more practice. Usually there are only one or two questions on this section that contain such subtle distinctions that you're unable to answer confidently, and you then may find yourself stuck deciding between two possible choices, neither of which you're sure about.

EXAMINATION SECTION
TEST 1

DIRECTIONS: Each question consists of several sentences which can be arranged in a logical sequence. For each question, select the choice which places the numbered sentences in the MOST logical sequence. *PRINT THE LETTER OF THE CORRECT ANSWER IN THE SPACE AT THE RIGHT.*

1. I. A body was found in the woods.
    II. A man proclaimed innocence.
    III. The owner of a gun was located.
    IV. A gun was traced.
    V. The owner of a gun was questioned.
    The CORRECT answer is:

    A. IV, III, V, II, I
    B. II, I, IV, III, V
    C. I, IV, III, V, II
    D. I, III, V, II, IV
    E. I, II, IV, III, V

2. I. A man was in a hunting accident.
    II. A man fell down a flight of steps.
    III. A man lost his vision in one eye.
    IV. A man broke his leg.
    V. A man had to walk with a cane.
    The CORRECT answer is:

    A. II, IV, V, I, III
    B. IV, V, I, III, II
    C. III, I, IV, V, II
    D. I, III, V, II, IV
    E. I, III, II, IV, V

3. I. A man is offered a new job.
    II. A woman is offered a new job.
    III. A man works as a waiter.
    IV. A woman works as a waitress.
    V. A woman gives notice.
    The CORRECT answer is:

    A. IV, II, V, III, I
    B. IV, II, V, I, III
    C. II, IV, V, III, I
    D. III, I, IV, II, V
    E. IV, III, II, V, I

4. I. A train left the station late.
    II. A man was late for work.
    III. A man lost his job.
    IV. Many people complained because the train was late.
    V. There was a traffic jam.
    The CORRECT answer is:

    A. V, II, I, IV, III
    B. V, I, IV, II, III
    C. V, I, II, IV, III
    D. I, V, IV, II, III
    E. II, I, IV, V, III

1. ____

2. ____

3. ____

4. ____

5.
I. The burden of proof as to each issue is determined before trial and remains upon the same party throughout the trial.
II. The jury is at liberty to believe one witness' testimony as against a number of contradictory witnesses.
III. In a civil case, the party bearing the burden of proof is required to prove his contention by a fair preponderance of the evidence.
IV. However, it must be noted that a fair preponderance of evidence does not necessarily mean a greater number of witnesses.
V. The burden of proof is the burden which rests upon one of the parties to an action to persuade the trier of the facts, generally the jury, that a proposition he asserts is true.
VI. If the evidence is equally balanced, or if it leaves the jury in such doubt as to be unable to decide the controversy either way, judgment must be given against the party upon whom the burden of proof rests.

The CORRECT answer is:

A. III, II, V, IV, I, VI
B. I, II, VI, V, III, IV
C. III, IV, V, I, II, VI
D. V, I, III, VI, IV, II
E. I, V, III, VI, IV, II

6.
I. If a parent is without assets and is unemployed, he cannot be convicted of the crime of non-support of a child.
II. The term *sufficient ability* has been held to mean sufficient financial ability.
III. It does not matter if his unemployment is by choice or unavoidable circumstances.
IV. If he fails to take any steps at all, he may be liable to prosecution for endangering the welfare of a child.
V. Under the penal law, a parent is responsible for the support of his minor child only if the parent is of *sufficient ability*.
VI. An indigent parent may meet his obligation by borrowing money or by seeking aid under the provisions of the Social Welfare Law.

The CORRECT answer is:

A. VI, I, V, III, II, IV
B. I, III, V, II, IV, VI
C. V, II, I, III, VI, IV
D. I, VI, IV, V, II, III
E. II, V, I, III, VI, IV

7.
I. Consider, for example, the case of a rabble rouser who urges a group of twenty people to go out and break the windows of a nearby factory.
II. Therefore, the law fills the indicated gap with the crime of *inciting to riot*.
III. A person is considered guilty of inciting to riot when he urges ten or more persons to engage in tumultuous and violent conduct of a kind likely to create public alarm.
IV. However, if he has not obtained the cooperation of at least four people, he cannot be charged with unlawful assembly.
V. The charge of inciting to riot was added to the law to cover types of conduct which cannot be classified as either the crime of *riot* or the crime of *unlawful assembly*.
VI. If he acquires the acquiescence of at least four of them, he is guilty of unlawful assembly even if the project does not materialize.

The CORRECT answer is:

A. III, V, I, VI, IV, II   B. V, I, IV, VI, II, III
C. III, IV, I, V, II, VI   D. V, I, IV, VI, III, II
E. V, III, I, VI, IV, II

8.   I.   If, however, the rebuttal evidence presents an issue of credibility, it is for the jury to determine whether the presumption has, in fact, been destroyed.
     II. Once sufficient evidence to the contrary is introduced, the presumption disappears from the trial.
     III. The effect of a presumption is to place the burden upon the adversary to come forward with evidence to rebut the presumption.
     IV. When a presumption is overcome and ceases to exist in the case, the fact or facts which gave rise to the presumption still remain.
     V.   Whether a presumption has been overcome is ordinarily a question for the court.
     VI. Such information may furnish a basis for a logical inference.
     The CORRECT answer is:

     A. IV, VI, II, V, I, III   B. III, II, V, I, IV, VI
     C. V, III, VI, IV, II, I   D. V, IV, I, II, VI, III
     E. II, III, V, I, IV, VI

9.   I.   An executive may answer a letter by writing his reply on the face of the letter itself instead of having a return letter typed.
     II. This procedure is efficient because it saves the executive's time, the typist's time, and saves office file space.
     III. Copying machines are used in small offices as well as large offices to save time and money in making brief replies to business letters.
     IV. A copy is made on a copying machine to go into the company files, while the original is mailed back to the sender.
     The CORRECT answer is:

     A. I, II, IV, III   B. I, IV, II, III
     C. III, I, IV, II   D. III, IV, II, I

10. I.   Most organizations favor one of the types but always include the others to a lesser degree.
     II. However, we can detect a definite trend toward greater use of symbolic control.
     III. We suggest that our local police agencies are today primarily utilizing material control.
     IV. Control can be classified into three types: physical, material, and symbolic.
     The CORRECT answer is:

     A. IV, II, III, I   B. II, I, IV, III
     C. III, IV, II, I   D. IV, I, III, II

11. I.   Project residents had first claim to this use, followed by surrounding neighborhood children.
     II. By contrast, recreation space within the project's interior was found to be used more often by both groups.
     III. Studies of the use of project grounds in many cities showed grounds left open for public use were neglected and unused, both by residents and by members of the surrounding community.

IV. Project residents had clearly laid claim to the play spaces, setting up and enforcing unwritten rules for use.
V. Each group, by experience, found their activities easily disrupted by other groups, and their claim to the use of space for recreation difficult to enforce.

The CORRECT answer is:

A. IV, V, I, II, III
B. V, II, IV, III, I
C. I, IV, III, II, V
D. III, V, II, IV, I

12.
I. They do not consider the problems correctable within the existing subsidy formula and social policy of accepting all eligible applicants regardless of social behavior and lifestyle.
II. A recent survey, however, indicated that tenants believe these problems correctable by local housing authorities and management within the existing financial formula.
III. Many of the problems and complaints concerning public housing management and design have created resentment between the tenant and the landlord.
IV. This same survey indicated that administrators and managers do not agree with the tenants.

The CORRECT answer is:

A. II, I, III, IV
B. I, III, IV, II
C. III, II, IV, I
D. IV, II, I, III

13.
I. In single-family residences, there is usually enough distance between tenants to prevent occupants from annoying one another.
II. For example, a certain small percentage of tenant families has one or more members addicted to alcohol.
III. While managers believe in the right of individuals to live as they choose, the manager becomes concerned when the pattern of living jeopardizes others' rights.
IV. Still others turn night into day, staging lusty entertainments which carry on into the hours when most tenants are trying to sleep.
V. In apartment buildings, however, tenants live so closely together that any misbehavior can result in unpleasant living conditions.
VI. Other families engage in violent argument.

The CORRECT answer is:

A. III, II, V, IV, VI, I
B. I, V, II, VI, IV, III
C. II, V, IV, I, III, VI
D. IV, II, V, VI, III, I

14.
I. Congress made the commitment explicit in the Housing Act of 1949, establishing as a national goal the realization of *a decent home and suitable environment for every American family.*
II. The result has been that the goal of decent home and suitable environment is still as far distant as ever for the disadvantaged urban family.
III. In spite of this action by Congress, federal housing programs have continued to be fragmented and grossly underfunded.
IV. The passage of the National Housing Act signalled a new federal commitment to provide housing for the nation's citizens.

The CORRECT answer is:

A. I, IV, III, II
B. IV, I, III, II
C. IV, I, II, III
D. II, IV, I, III

15.
I. The greater expense does not necessarily involve *exploitation,* but it is often perceived as exploitative and unfair by those who are aware of the price differences involved, but unaware of operating costs.
II. Ghetto residents believe they are *exploited* by local merchants, and evidence substantiates some of these beliefs.
III. However, stores in low-income areas were more likely to be small independents, which could not achieve the economies available to supermarket chains and were, therefore, more likely to charge higher prices, and the customers were more likely to buy smaller-sized packages which are more expensive per unit of measure.
IV. A study conducted in one city showed that distinctly higher prices were charged for goods sold in ghetto stores than in other areas.

The CORRECT answer is:

A. IV, II, I, III
C. II, IV, III, I
B. IV, I, III, II
D. II, III, IV, I

15._____

KEY (CORRECT ANSWERS)

1. C
2. E
3. B
4. B
5. D

6. C
7. A
8. B
9. C
10. D

11. D
12. C
13. B
14. B
15. C

GLOSSARY OF LEGAL TERMS

TABLE OF CONTENTS

	Page
Action ... Affiant	1
Affidavit ... At Bar	2
At Issue ... Burden of Proof	3
Business ... Commute	4
Complainant ... Conviction	5
Cooperative ... Demur (v.)	6
Demurrage ... Endorsement	7
Enjoin ... Facsimile	8
Factor ... Guilty	9
Habeas Corpus ... Incumbrance	10
Indemnify ... Laches	11
Landlord and Tenant ... Malice	12
Mandamus ... Obiter Dictum	13
Object (v.) ... Perjury	14
Perpetuity ... Proclamation	15
Proffered Evidence ... Referee	16
Referendum ... Stare Decisis	17
State ... Term	18
Testamentary ... Warrant (Warranty) (v.)	19
Warrant (n.) ... Zoning	20

GLOSSARY OF LEGAL TERMS

A

ACTION - "Action" includes a civil action and a criminal action.
A FORTIORI - A term meaning you can reason one thing from the existence of certain facts.
A POSTERIORI - From what goes after; from effect to cause.
A PRIORI - From what goes before; from cause to effect.
AB INITIO - From the beginning.
ABATE - To diminish or put an end to.
ABET - To encourage the commission of a crime.
ABEYANCE - Suspension, temporary suppression.
ABIDE - To accept the consequences of.
ABJURE - To renounce; give up.
ABRIDGE - To reduce; contract; diminish.
ABROGATE - To annul, repeal, or destroy.
ABSCOND - To hide or absent oneself to avoid legal action.
ABSTRACT - A summary.
ABUT - To border on, to touch.
ACCESS - Approach; in real property law it means the right of the owner of property to the use of the highway or road next to his land, without obstruction by intervening property owners.
ACCESSORY - In criminal law, it means the person who contributes or aids in the commission of a crime.
ACCOMMODATED PARTY - One to whom credit is extended on the strength of another person signing a commercial paper.
ACCOMMODATION PAPER - A commercial paper to which the accommodating party has put his name.
ACCOMPLICE - In criminal law, it means a person who together with the principal offender commits a crime.
ACCORD - An agreement to accept something different or less than that to which one is entitled, which extinguishes the entire obligation.
ACCOUNT - A statement of mutual demands in the nature of debt and credit between parties.
ACCRETION - The act of adding to a thing; in real property law, it means gradual accumulation of land by natural causes.
ACCRUE - To grow to; to be added to.
ACKNOWLEDGMENT - The act of going before an official authorized to take acknowledgments, and acknowledging an act as one's own.
ACQUIESCENCE - A silent appearance of consent.
ACQUIT - To legally determine the innocence of one charged with a crime.
AD INFINITUM - Indefinitely.
AD LITEM - For the suit.
AD VALOREM - According to value.
ADJECTIVE LAW - Rules of procedure.
ADJUDICATION - The judgment given in a case.
ADMIRALTY - Court having jurisdiction over maritime cases.
ADULT - Sixteen years old or over (in criminal law).
ADVANCE - In commercial law, it means to pay money or render other value before it is due.
ADVERSE - Opposed; contrary.
ADVOCATE - (v.) To speak in favor of;
 (n.) One who assists, defends, or pleads for another.
AFFIANT - A person who makes and signs an affidavit.

AFFIDAVIT - A written and sworn to declaration of facts, voluntarily made.
AFFINITY- The relationship between persons through marriage with the kindred of each other; distinguished from consanguinity, which is the relationship by blood.
AFFIRM - To ratify; also when an appellate court affirms a judgment, decree, or order, it means that it is valid and right and must stand as rendered in the lower court.
AFOREMENTIONED; AFORESAID - Before or already said.
AGENT - One who represents and acts for another.
AID AND COMFORT - To help; encourage.
ALIAS - A name not one's true name.
ALIBI - A claim of not being present at a certain place at a certain time.
ALLEGE - To assert.
ALLOTMENT - A share or portion.
AMBIGUITY - Uncertainty; capable of being understood in more than one way.
AMENDMENT - Any language made or proposed as a change in some principal writing.
AMICUS CURIAE - A friend of the court; one who has an interest in a case, although not a party in the case, who volunteers advice upon matters of law to the judge. For example, a brief amicus curiae.
AMORTIZATION - To provide for a gradual extinction of (a future obligation) in advance of maturity, especially, by periodical contributions to a sinking fund which will be adequate to discharge a debt or make a replacement when it becomes necessary.
ANCILLARY - Aiding, auxiliary.
ANNOTATION - A note added by way of comment or explanation.
ANSWER - A written statement made by a defendant setting forth the grounds of his defense.
ANTE - Before.
ANTE MORTEM - Before death.
APPEAL - The removal of a case from a lower court to one of superior jurisdiction for the purpose of obtaining a review.
APPEARANCE - Coming into court as a party to a suit.
APPELLANT - The party who takes an appeal from one court or jurisdiction to another (appellate) court for review.
APPELLEE - The party against whom an appeal is taken.
APPROPRIATE - To make a thing one's own.
APPROPRIATION - Prescribing the destination of a thing; the act of the legislature designating a particular fund, to be applied to some object of government expenditure.
APPURTENANT - Belonging to; accessory or incident to.
ARBITER - One who decides a dispute; a referee.
ARBITRARY - Unreasoned; not governed by any fixed rules or standard.
ARGUENDO - By way of argument.
ARRAIGN - To call the prisoner before the court to answer to a charge.
ASSENT - A declaration of willingness to do something in compliance with a request.
ASSERT - Declare.
ASSESS - To fix the rate or amount.
ASSIGN - To transfer; to appoint; to select for a particular purpose.
ASSIGNEE - One who receives an assignment.
ASSIGNOR - One who makes an assignment.
AT BAR - Before the court.

AT ISSUE - When parties in an action come to a point where one asserts something and the other denies it.
ATTACH - Seize property by court order and sometimes arrest a person.
ATTEST - To witness a will, etc.; act of attestation.
AVERMENT - A positive statement of facts.

B

BAIL - To obtain the release of a person from legal custody by giving security and promising that he shall appear in court; to deliver (goods, etc.) in trust to a person for a special purpose.
BAILEE - One to whom personal property is delivered under a contract of bailment.
BAILMENT - Delivery of personal property to another to be held for a certain purpose and to be returned when the purpose is accomplished.
BAILOR - The party who delivers goods to another, under a contract of bailment.
BANC (OR BANK) - Bench; the place where a court sits permanently or regularly; also the assembly of all the judges of a court.
BANKRUPT - An insolvent person, technically, one declared to be bankrupt after a bankruptcy proceeding.
BAR - The legal profession.
BARRATRY - Exciting groundless judicial proceedings.
BARTER - A contract by which parties exchange goods for other goods.
BATTERY - Illegal interfering with another's person.
BEARER - In commercial law, it means the person in possession of a commercial paper which is payable to the bearer.
BENCH - The court itself or the judge.
BENEFICIARY - A person benefiting under a will, trust, or agreement.
BEST EVIDENCE RULE, THE - Except as otherwise provided by statute, no evidence other than the writing itself is admissible to prove the content of a writing. This section shall be known and may be cited as the best evidence rule.
BEQUEST - A gift of personal property under a will.
BILL - A formal written statement of complaint to a court of justice; also, a draft of an act of the legislature before it becomes a law; also, accounts for goods sold, services rendered, or work done.
BONA FIDE - In or with good faith; honestly.
BOND - An instrument by which the maker promises to pay a sum of money to another, usually providing that upon performances of a certain condition the obligation shall be void.
BOYCOTT - A plan to prevent the carrying on of a business by wrongful means.
BREACH - The breaking or violating of a law, or the failure to carry out a duty.
BRIEF - A written document, prepared by a lawyer to serve as the basis of an argument upon a case in court, usually an appellate court.
BURDEN OF PRODUCING EVIDENCE - The obligation of a party to introduce evidence sufficient to avoid a ruling against him on the issue.
BURDEN OF PROOF - The obligation of a party to establish by evidence a requisite degree of belief concerning a fact in the mind of the trier of fact or the court. The burden of proof may require a party to raise a reasonable doubt concerning the existence of nonexistence of a fact or that he establish the existence or nonexistence of a fact by a preponderance of the evidence, by clear and convincing proof, or by proof beyond a reasonable doubt.

Except as otherwise provided by law, the burden of proof requires proof by a preponderance of the evidence.

BUSINESS, A - Shall include every kind of business, profession, occupation, calling or operation of institutions, whether carried on for profit or not.

BY-LAWS - Regulations, ordinances, or rules enacted by a corporation, association, etc., for its own government.

C

CANON - A doctrine; also, a law or rule, of a church or association in particular.

CAPIAS - An order to arrest.

CAPTION - In a pleading, deposition or other paper connected with a case in court, it is the heading or introductory clause which shows the names of the parties, name of the court, number of the case on the docket or calendar, etc.

CARRIER - A person or corporation undertaking to transport persons or property.

CASE - A general term for an action, cause, suit, or controversy before a judicial body.

CAUSE - A suit, litigation or action before a court.

CAVEAT EMPTOR - Let the buyer beware. This term expresses the rule that the purchaser of an article must examine, judge, and test it for himself, being bound to discover any obvious defects or imperfections.

CERTIFICATE - A written representation that some legal formality has been complied with.

CERTIORARI - To be informed of; the name of a writ issued by a superior court directing the lower court to send up to the former the record and proceedings of a case.

CHANGE OF VENUE - To remove place of trial from one place to another.

CHARGE - An obligation or duty; a formal complaint; an instruction of the court to the jury upon a case.

CHARTER - (n.) The authority by virtue of which an organized body acts;
(v.) in mercantile law, it means to hire or lease a vehicle or vessel for transportation.

CHATTEL - An article of personal property.

CHATTEL MORTGAGE - A mortgage on personal property.

CIRCUIT - A division of the country, for the administration of justice; a geographical area served by a court.

CITATION - The act of the court by which a person is summoned or cited; also, a reference to legal authority.

CIVIL (ACTIONS)- It indicates the private rights and remedies of individuals in contrast to the word "criminal" (actions) which relates to prosecution for violation of laws.

CLAIM (n.) - Any demand held or asserted as of right.

CODICIL - An addition to a will.

CODIFY - To arrange the laws of a country into a code.

COGNIZANCE - Notice or knowledge.

COLLATERAL - By the side; accompanying; an article or thing given to secure performance of a promise.

COMITY - Courtesy; the practice by which one court follows the decision of another court on the same question.

COMMIT - To perform, as an act; to perpetrate, as a crime; to send a person to prison.

COMMON LAW - As distinguished from law created by the enactment of the legislature (called statutory law), it relates to those principles and rules of action which derive their authority solely from usages and customs of immemorial antiquity, particularly with reference to the ancient unwritten law of England. The written pronouncements of the common law are found in court decisions.

COMMUTE - Change punishment to one less severe.

COMPLAINANT - One who applies to the court for legal redress.
COMPLAINT - The pleading of a plaintiff in a civil action; or a charge that a person has committed a specified offense.
COMPROMISE - An arrangement for settling a dispute by agreement.
CONCUR - To agree, consent.
CONCURRENT - Running together, at the same time.
CONDEMNATION - Taking private property for public use on payment therefor.
CONDITION - Mode or state of being; a qualification or restriction.
CONDUCT - Active and passive behavior; both verbal and nonverbal.
CONFESSION - Voluntary statement of guilt of crime.
CONFIDENTIAL COMMUNICATION BETWEEN CLIENT AND LAWYER - Information transmitted between a client and his lawyer in the course of that relationship and in confidence by a means which, so far as the client is aware, discloses the information to no third persons other than those who are present to further the interest of the client in the consultation or those to whom disclosure is reasonably necessary for the transmission of the information or the accomplishment of the purpose for which the lawyer is consulted, and includes a legal opinion formed and the advice given by the lawyer in the course of that relationship.
CONFRONTATION - Witness testifying in presence of defendant.
CONSANGUINITY - Blood relationship.
CONSIGN - To give in charge; commit; entrust; to send or transmit goods to a merchant, factor, or agent for sale.
CONSIGNEE - One to whom a consignment is made.
CONSIGNOR - One who sends or makes a consignment.
CONSPIRACY - In criminal law, it means an agreement between two or more persons to commit an unlawful act.
CONSPIRATORS - Persons involved in a conspiracy.
CONSTITUTION - The fundamental law of a nation or state.
CONSTRUCTION OF GENDERS - The masculine gender includes the feminine and neuter.
CONSTRUCTION OF SINGULAR AND PLURAL - The singular number includes the plural; and the plural, the singular.
CONSTRUCTION OF TENSES - The present tense includes the past and future tenses; and the future, the present.
CONSTRUCTIVE - An act or condition assumed from other parts or conditions.
CONSTRUE - To ascertain the meaning of language.
CONSUMMATE - To complete.
CONTIGUOUS - Adjoining; touching; bounded by.
CONTINGENT - Possible, but not assured; dependent upon some condition.
CONTINUANCE - The adjournment or postponement of an action pending in a court.
CONTRA - Against, opposed to; contrary.
CONTRACT - An agreement between two or more persons to do or not to do a particular thing.
CONTROVERT - To dispute, deny.
CONVERSION - Dealing with the personal property of another as if it were one's own, without right.
CONVEYANCE - An instrument transferring title to land.
CONVICTION - Generally, the result of a criminal trial which ends in a judgment or sentence that the defendant is guilty as charged.

COOPERATIVE - A cooperative is a voluntary organization of persons with a common interest, formed and operated along democratic lines for the purpose of supplying services at cost to its members and other patrons, who contribute both capital and business.
CORPUS DELICTI - The body of a crime; the crime itself.
CORROBORATE - To strengthen; to add weight by additional evidence.
COUNTERCLAIM - A claim presented by a defendant in opposition to or deduction from the claim of the plaintiff.
COUNTY - Political subdivision of a state.
COVENANT - Agreement.
CREDIBLE - Worthy of belief.
CREDITOR - A person to whom a debt is owing by another person, called the "debtor."
CRIMINAL ACTION - Includes criminal proceedings.
CRIMINAL INFORMATION - Same as complaint.
CRITERION (sing.)
CRITERIA (plural) - A means or tests for judging; a standard or standards.
CROSS-EXAMINATION - Examination of a witness by a party other than the direct examiner upon a matter that is within the scope of the direct examination of the witness.
CULPABLE - Blamable.
CY-PRES - As near as (possible). The rule of *cy-pres* is a rule for the construction of instruments in equity by which the intention of the party is carried out *as near as may be*, when it would be impossible or illegal to give it literal effect.

D

DAMAGES - A monetary compensation, which may be recovered in the courts by any person who has suffered loss, or injury, whether to his person, property or rights through the unlawful act or omission or negligence of another.
DECLARANT - A person who makes a statement.
DE FACTO - In fact; actually but without legal authority.
DE JURE - Of right; legitimate; lawful.
DE MINIMIS - Very small or trifling.
DE NOVO - Anew; afresh; a second time.
DEBT - A specified sum of money owing to one person from another, including not only the obligation of the debtor to pay, but the right of the creditor to receive and enforce payment.
DECEDENT - A dead person.
DECISION - A judgment or decree pronounced by a court in determination of a case.
DECREE - An order of the court, determining the rights of all parties to a suit.
DEED - A writing containing a contract sealed and delivered; particularly to convey real property.
DEFALCATION - Misappropriation of funds.
DEFAMATION - Injuring one's reputation by false statements.
DEFAULT - The failure to fulfill a duty, observe a promise, discharge an obligation, or perform an agreement.
DEFENDANT - The person defending or denying; the party against whom relief or recovery is sought in an action or suit.
DEFRAUD - To practice fraud; to cheat or trick.
DELEGATE (v.)- To entrust to the care or management of another.
DELICTUS - A crime.
DEMUR (v.) - To dispute the sufficiency in law of the pleading of the other side.

DEMURRAGE - In maritime law, it means, the sum fixed or allowed as remuneration to the owners of a ship for the detention of their vessel beyond the number of days allowed for loading and unloading or for sailing; also used in railroad terminology.
DENIAL - A form of pleading; refusing to admit the truth of a statement, charge, etc.
DEPONENT - One who gives testimony under oath reduced to writing.
DEPOSITION - Testimony given under oath outside of court for use in court or for the purpose of obtaining information in preparation for trial of a case.
DETERIORATION - A degeneration such as from decay, corrosion or disintegration.
DETRIMENT - Any loss or harm to person or property.
DEVIATION - A turning aside.
DEVISE - A gift of real property by the last will and testament of the donor.
DICTUM (sing.)
DICTA (plural) - Any statements made by the court in an opinion concerning some rule of law not necessarily involved nor essential to the determination of the case.
DIRECT EVIDENCE - Evidence that directly proves a fact, without an inference or presumption, and which in itself if true, conclusively establishes that fact.
DIRECT EXAMINATION - The first examination of a witness upon a matter that is not within the scope of a previous examination of the witness.
DISAFFIRM - To repudiate.
DISMISS - In an action or suit, it means to dispose of the case without any further consideration or hearing.
DISSENT - To denote disagreement of one or more judges of a court with the decision passed by the majority upon a case before them.
DOCKET (n.) - A formal record, entered in brief, of the proceedings in a court.
DOCTRINE - A rule, principle, theory of law.
DOMICILE - That place where a man has his true, fixed and permanent home to which whenever he is absent he has the intention of returning.
DRAFT (n.) - A commercial paper ordering payment of money drawn by one person on another.
DRAWEE - The person who is requested to pay the money.
DRAWER - The person who draws the commercial paper and addresses it to the drawee.
DUPLICATE - A counterpart produced by the same impression as the original enlargements and miniatures, or by mechanical or electronic re-recording, or by chemical reproduction, or by other equivalent technique which accurately reproduces the original.
DURESS - Use of force to compel performance or non-performance of an act.

E

EASEMENT - A liberty, privilege, or advantage without profit, in the lands of another.
EGRESS - Act or right of going out or leaving; emergence.
EIUSDEM GENERIS - Of the same kind, class or nature. A rule used in the construction of language in a legal document.
EMBEZZLEMENT - To steal; to appropriate fraudulently to one's own use property entrusted to one's care.
EMBRACERY - Unlawful attempt to influence jurors, etc., but not by offering value.
EMINENT DOMAIN - The right of a state to take private property for public use.
ENACT - To make into a law.
ENDORSEMENT - Act of writing one's name on the back of a note, bill or similar written instrument.

ENJOIN - To require a person, by writ of injunction from a court of equity, to perform or to abstain or desist from some act.
ENTIRETY - The whole; that which the law considers as one whole, and not capable of being divided into parts.
ENTRAPMENT - Inducing one to commit a crime so as to arrest him.
ENUMERATED - Mentioned specifically; designated.
ENURE - To operate or take effect.
EQUITY - In its broadest sense, this term denotes the spirit and the habit of fairness, justness, and right dealing which regulate the conduct of men.
ERROR - A mistake of law, or the false or irregular application of law as will nullify the judicial proceedings.
ESCROW - A deed, bond or other written engagement, delivered to a third person, to be delivered by him only upon the performance or fulfillment of some condition.
ESTATE - The interest which any one has in lands, or in any other subject of property.
ESTOP - To stop, bar, or impede.
ESTOPPEL - A rule of law which prevents a man from alleging or denying a fact, because of his own previous act.
ET AL. (alii) - And others.
ET SEQ. (sequential) - And the following.
ET UX. (uxor) - And wife.
EVIDENCE - Testimony, writings, material objects, or other things presented to the senses that are offered to prove the existence or non-existence of a fact.
      Means from which inferences may be drawn as a basis of proof in duly constituted judicial or fact finding tribunals, and includes testimony in the form of opinion and hearsay.
EX CONTRACTU
EX DELICTO - In law, rights and causes of action are divided into two classes, those arising *ex contractu* (from a contract) and those arising *ex delicto* (from a delict or tort).
EX OFFICIO - From office; by virtue of the office.
EX PARTE - On one side only; by or for one.
EX POST FACTO - After the fact.
EX POST FACTO LAW - A law passed after an act was done which retroactively makes such act a crime.
EX REL. (relations) - Upon relation or information.
EXCEPTION - An objection upon a matter of law to a decision made, either before or after judgment by a court.
EXECUTOR (male)
EXECUTRIX (female) - A person who has been appointed by will to execute the will.
EXECUTORY - That which is yet to be executed or performed.
EXEMPT - To release from some liability to which others are subject.
EXONERATION - The removal of a burden, charge or duty.
EXTRADITION - Surrender of a fugitive from one nation to another.

F

F.A.S.- "Free alongside ship"; delivery at dock for ship named.
F.O.B.- "Free on board"; seller will deliver to car, truck, vessel, or other conveyance by which goods are to be transported, without expense or risk of loss to the buyer or consignee.
FABRICATE - To construct; to invent a false story.
FACSIMILE - An exact or accurate copy of an original instrument.

FACTOR - A commercial agent.
FEASANCE - The doing of an act.
FELONIOUS - Criminal, malicious.
FELONY - Generally, a criminal offense that may be punished by death or imprisonment for more than one year as differentiated from a misdemeanor.
FEME SOLE - A single woman.
FIDUCIARY - A person who is invested with rights and powers to be exercised for the benefit of another person.
FIERI FACIAS - A writ of execution commanding the sheriff to levy and collect the amount of a judgment from the goods and chattels of the judgment debtor.
FINDING OF FACT - Determination from proof or judicial notice of the existence of a fact. A ruling implies a supporting finding of fact; no separate or formal finding is required unless required by a statute of this state.
FISCAL - Relating to accounts or the management of revenue.
FORECLOSURE (sale) - A sale of mortgaged property to obtain satisfaction of the mortgage out of the sale proceeds.
FORFEITURE - A penalty, a fine.
FORGERY - Fabricating or producing falsely, counterfeited.
FORTUITOUS - Accidental.
FORUM - A court of justice; a place of jurisdiction.
FRAUD - Deception; trickery.
FREEHOLDER - One who owns real property.
FUNGIBLE - Of such kind or nature that one specimen or part may be used in the place of another.

G

GARNISHEE - Person garnished.
GARNISHMENT - A legal process to reach the money or effects of a defendant, in the possession or control of a third person.
GRAND JURY - Not less than 16, not more than 23 citizens of a county sworn to inquire into crimes committed or triable in the county.
GRANT - To agree to; convey, especially real property.
GRANTEE - The person to whom a grant is made.
GRANTOR - The person by whom a grant is made.
GRATUITOUS - Given without a return, compensation or consideration.
GRAVAMEN - The grievance complained of or the substantial cause of a criminal action.
GUARANTY (n.) - A promise to answer for the payment of some debt, or the performance of some duty, in case of the failure of another person, who, in the first instance, is liable for such payment or performance.
GUARDIAN - The person, committee, or other representative authorized by law to protect the person or estate or both of an incompetent (or of a *sui juris* person having a guardian) and to act for him in matters affecting his person or property or both. An incompetent is a person under disability imposed by law.
GUILTY - Establishment of the fact that one has committed a breach of conduct; especially, a violation of law.

H

HABEAS CORPUS - You have the body; the name given to a variety of writs, having for their object to bring a party before a court or judge for decision as to whether such person is being lawfully held prisoner.
HABENDUM - In conveyancing; it is the clause in a deed conveying land which defines the extent of ownership to be held by the grantee.
HEARING - A proceeding whereby the arguments of the interested parties are heared.
HEARSAY - A type of testimony given by a witness who relates, not what he knows personally, but what others have told hi, or what he has heard said by others.
HEARSAY RULE, THE - (a) "Hearsay evidence" is evidence of a statement that was made other than by a witness while testifying at the hearing and that is offered to prove the truth of the matter stated; (b) Except as provided by law, hearsay evidence is inadmissible; (c) This section shall be known and may be cited as the hearsay rule.
HEIR - Generally, one who inherits property, real or personal.
HOLDER OF THE PRIVILEGE - (a) The client when he has no guardian or conservator; (b) A guardian or conservator of the client when the client has a guardian or conservator; (c) The personal representative of the client if the client is dead; (d) A successor, assign, trustee in dissolution, or any similar representative of a firm, association, organization, partnership, business trust, corporation, or public entity that is no longer in existence.
HUNG JURY - One so divided that they can't agree on a verdict.
HUSBAND-WIFE PRIVILEGE - An accused in a criminal proceeding has a privilege to prevent his spouse from testifying against him.
HYPOTHECATE - To pledge a thing without delivering it to the pledgee.
HYPOTHESIS - A supposition, assumption, or toehry.

I

I.E. (id est) - That is.
IB., OR IBID.(ibidem) - In the same place; used to refer to a legal reference previously cited to avoid repeating the entire citation.
ILLICIT - Prohibited; unlawful.
ILLUSORY - Deceiving by false appearance.
IMMUNITY - Exemption.
IMPEACH - To accuse, to dispute.
IMPEDIMENTS - Disabilities, or hindrances.
IMPLEAD - To sue or prosecute by due course of law.
IMPUTED - Attributed or charged to.
IN LOCO PARENTIS - In place of parent, a guardian.
IN TOTO - In the whole; completely.
INCHOATE - Imperfect; unfinished.
INCOMMUNICADO - Denial of the right of a prisoner to communicate with friends or relatives.
INCOMPETENT - One who is incapable of caring for his own affairs because he is mentally deficient or undeveloped.
INCRIMINATION - A matter will incriminate a person if it constitutes, or forms an essential part of, or, taken in connection with other matters disclosed, is a basis for a reasonable inference of such a violation of the laws of this State as to subject him to liability to punishment therefor, unless he has become for any reason permanently immune from punishment for such violation.
INCUMBRANCE - Generally a claim, lien, charge or liability attached to and binding real property.

INDEMNIFY - To secure against loss or damage; also, to make reimbursement to one for a loss already incurred by him.
INDEMNITY - An agreement to reimburse another person in case of an anticipated loss falling upon him.
INDICIA - Signs; indications.
INDICTMENT - An accusation in writing found and presented by a grand jury charging that a person has committed a crime.
INDORSE - To write a name on the back of a legal paper or document, generally, a negotiable instrument
INDUCEMENT - Cause or reason why a thing is done or that which incites the person to do the act or commit a crime; the motive for the criminal act.
INFANT - In civil cases one under 21 years of age.
INFORMATION - A formal accusation of crime made by a prosecuting attorney.
INFRA - Below, under; this word occurring by itself in a publication refers the reader to a future part of the publication.
INGRESS - The act of going into.
INJUNCTION - A writ or order by the court requiring a person, generally, to do or to refrain from doing an act.
INSOLVENT - The condition of a person who is unable to pay his debts.
INSTRUCTION - A direction given by the judge to the jury concerning the law of the case.
INTERIM - In the meantime; time intervening.
INTERLOCUTORY - Temporary, not final; something intervening between the commencement and the end of a suit which decides some point or matter, but is not a final decision of the whole controversy.
INTERROGATORIES - A series of formal written questions used in the examination of a party or a witness usually prior to a trial.
INTESTATE - A person who dies without a will.
INURE - To result, to take effect.
IPSO FACTO - By the fact iself; by the mere fact.
ISSUE (n.) The disputed point or question in a case,

J

JEOPARDY - Danger, hazard, peril.
JOINDER - Joining; uniting with another person in some legal steps or proceeding.
JOINT - United; combined.
JUDGE - Member or members or representative or representatives of a court conducting a trial or hearing at which evidence is introduced.
JUDGMENT - The official decision of a court of justice.
JUDICIAL OR JUDICIARY - Relating to or connected with the administration of justice.
JURAT - The clause written at the foot of an affidavit, stating when, where and before whom such affidavit was sworn.
JURISDICTION - The authority to hear and determine controversies between parties.
JURISPRUDENCE - The philosophy of law.
JURY - A body of persons legally selected to inquire into any matter of fact, and to render their verdict according to the evidence.

L

LACHES - The failure to diligently assert a right, which results in a refusal to allow relief.

LANDLORD AND TENANT - A phrase used to denote the legal relation existing between the owner and occupant of real estate.

LARCENY - Stealing personal property belonging to another.

LATENT - Hidden; that which does not appear on the face of a thing.

LAW - Includes constitutional, statutory, and decisional law.

LAWYER-CLIENT PRIVILEGE - (1) A "client" is a person, public officer, or corporation, association, or other organization or entity, either public or private, who is rendered professional legal services by a lawyer, or who consults a lawyer with a view to obtaining professional legal services from him; (2) A "lawyer" is a person authorized, or reasonably believed by the client to be authorized, to practice law in any state or nation; (3) A "representative of the lawyer" is one employed to assist the lawyer in the rendition of professional legal services; (4) A communication is "confidential" if not intended to be disclosed to third persons other than those to whom disclosure is in furtherance of the rendition of professional legal services to the client or those reasonably necessary for the transmission of the communication.

General rule of privilege - A client has a privilege to refuse to disclose and to prevent any other person from disclosing confidential communications made for the purpose of facilitating the rendition of professional legal services to the client, (1) between himself or his representative and his lawyer or his lawyer's representative, or (2) between his lawyer and the lawyer's representative, or (3) by him or his lawyer to a lawyer representing another in a matter of common interest, or (4) between representatives of the client or between the client and a representative of the client, or (5) between lawyers representing the client.

LEADING QUESTION - Question that suggests to the witness the answer that the examining party desires.

LEASE - A contract by which one conveys real estate for a limited time usually for a specified rent; personal property also may be leased.

LEGISLATION - The act of enacting laws.

LEGITIMATE - Lawful.

LESSEE - One to whom a lease is given.

LESSOR - One who grants a lease

LEVY - A collecting or exacting by authority.

LIABLE - Responsible; bound or obligated in law or equity.

LIBEL (v.) - To defame or injure a person's reputation by a published writing.

(n.) - The initial pleading on the part of the plaintiff in an admiralty proceeding.

LIEN - A hold or claim which one person has upon the property of another as a security for some debt or charge.

LIQUIDATED - Fixed; settled.

LIS PENDENS - A pending civil or criminal action.

LITERAL - According to the language.

LITIGANT - A party to a lawsuit.

LITATION - A judicial controversy.

LOCUS - A place.

LOCUS DELICTI - Place of the crime.

LOCUS POENITENTIAE - The abandoning or giving up of one's intention to commit some crime before it is fully completed or abandoning a conspiracy before its purpose is accomplished.

M

MALFEASANCE - To do a wrongful act.

MALICE - The doing of a wrongful act Intentionally without just cause or excuse.

MANDAMUS - The name of a writ issued by a court to enforce the performance of some public duty.
MANDATORY (adj.) Containing a command.
MARITIME - Pertaining to the sea or to commerce thereon.
MARSHALING - Arranging or disposing of in order.
MAXIM - An established principle or proposition.
MINISTERIAL - That which involves obedience to instruction, but demands no special discretion, judgment or skill.
MISAPPROPRIATE - Dealing fraudulently with property entrusted to one.
MISDEMEANOR - A crime less than a felony and punishable by a fine or imprisonment for less than one year.
MISFEASANCE - Improper performance of a lawful act.
MISREPRESENTATION - An untrue representation of facts.
MITIGATE - To make or become less severe, harsh.
MITTIMUS - A warrant of commitment to prison.
MOOT (adj.) Unsettled, undecided, not necessary to be decided.
MORTGAGE - A conveyance of property upon condition, as security for the payment of a debt or the performance of a duty, and to become void upon payment or performance according to the stipulated terms.
MORTGAGEE - A person to whom property is mortgaged.
MORTGAGOR - One who gives a mortgage.
MOTION - In legal proceedings, a "motion" is an application, either written or oral, addressed to the court by a party to an action or a suit requesting the ruling of the court on a matter of law.
MUTUALITY - Reciprocation.

N

NEGLIGENCE - The failure to exercise that degree of care which an ordinarily prudent person would exercise under like circumstances.
NEGOTIABLE (instrument) - Any instrument obligating the payment of money which is transferable from one person to another by endorsement and delivery or by delivery only.
NEGOTIATE - To transact business; to transfer a negotiable instrument; to seek agreement for the amicable disposition of a controversy or case.
NOLLE PROSEQUI - A formal entry upon the record, by the plaintiff in a civil suit or the prosecuting officer in a criminal action, by which he declares that he "will no further prosecute" the case.
NOLO CONTENDERE - The name of a plea in a criminal action, having the same effect as a plea of guilty; but not constituting a direct admission of guilt.
NOMINAL - Not real or substantial.
NOMINAL DAMAGES - Award of a trifling sum where no substantial injury is proved to have been sustained.
NONFEASANCE - Neglect of duty.
NOVATION - The substitution of a new debt or obligation for an existing one.
NUNC PRO TUNC - A phrase applied to acts allowed to be done after the time when they should be done, with a retroactive effect.("Now for then.")

O

OATH - Oath includes affirmation or declaration under penalty of perjury.
OBITER DICTUM - Opinion expressed by a court on a matter not essentially involved in a case and hence not a decision; also called dicta, if plural.

OBJECT (v.) - To oppose as improper or illegal and referring the question of its propriety or legality to the court.
OBLIGATION - A legal duty, by which a person is bound to do or not to do a certain thing.
OBLIGEE - The person to whom an obligation is owed.
OBLIGOR - The person who is to perform the obligation.
OFFER (v.) - To present for acceptance or rejection.
    (n.) - A proposal to do a thing, usually a proposal to make a contract.
OFFICIAL INFORMATION - Information within the custody or control of a department or agency of the government the disclosure of which is shown to be contrary to the public interest.
OFFSET - A deduction.
ONUS PROBANDI - Burden of proof.
OPINION - The statement by a judge of the decision reached in a case, giving the law as applied to the case and giving reasons for the judgment; also a belief or view.
OPTION - The exercise of the power of choice; also a privilege existing in one person, for which he has paid money, which gives him the right to buy or sell real or personal property at a given price within a specified time.
ORDER - A rule or regulation; every direction of a court or judge made or entered in writing but not including a judgment.
ORDINANCE - Generally, a rule established by authority; also commonly used to designate the legislative acts of a municipal corporation.
ORIGINAL - Writing or recording itself or any counterpart intended to have the same effect by a person executing or issuing it. An "original" of a photograph includes the negative or any print therefrom. If data are stored in a computer or similar device, any printout or other output readable by sight, shown to reflect the data accurately, is an "original."
OVERT - Open, manifest.

P

PANEL - A group of jurors selected to serve during a term of the court.
PARENS PATRIAE - Sovereign power of a state to protect or be a guardian over children and incompetents.
PAROL - Oral or verbal.
PAROLE - To release one in prison before the expiration of his sentence, conditionally.
PARITY - Equality in purchasing power between the farmer and other segments of the economy.
PARTITION - A legal division of real or personal property between one or more owners.
PARTNERSHIP - An association of two or more persons to carry on as co-owners a business for profit.
PATENT (adj.) - Evident.
    (n.) - A grant of some privilege, property, or authority, made by the government or sovereign of a country to one or more individuals.
PECULATION - Stealing.
PECUNIARY - Monetary.
PENULTIMATE - Next to the last.
PER CURIAM - A phrase used in the report of a decision to distinguish an opinion of the whole court from an opinion written by any one judge.
PER SE - In itself; taken alone.
PERCEIVE - To acquire knowledge through one's senses.
PEREMPTORY - Imperative; absolute.
PERJURY - To lie or state falsely under oath.

PERPETUITY - Perpetual existence; also the quality or condition of an estate limited so that it will not take effect or vest within the period fixed by law.
PERSON - Includes a natural person, firm, association, organization, partnership, business trust, corporation, or public entity.
PERSONAL PROPERTY - Includes money, goods, chattels, things in action, and evidences of debt.
PERSONALTY - Short term for personal property.
PETITION - An application in writing for an order of the court, stating the circumstances upon which it is founded and requesting any order or other relief from a court.
PLAINTIFF - A person who brings a court action.
PLEA - A pleading in a suit or action.
PLEADINGS - Formal allegations made by the parties of their respective claims and defenses, for the judgment of the court.
PLEDGE - A deposit of personal property as a security for the performance of an act.
PLEDGEE - The party to whom goods are delivered in pledge.
PLEDGOR - The party delivering goods in pledge.
PLENARY - Full; complete.
POLICE POWER - Inherent power of the state or its political subdivisions to enact laws within constitutional limits to promote the general welfare of society or the community.
POLLING THE JURY - Call the names of persons on a jury and requiring each juror to declare what his verdict is before it is legally recorded.
POST MORTEM - After death.
POWER OF ATTORNEY - A writing authorizing one to act for another.
PRECEPT - An order, warrant, or writ issued to an officer or body of officers, commanding him or them to do some act within the scope of his or their powers.
PRELIMINARY FACT - Fact upon the existence or nonexistence of which depends the admissibility or inadmissibility of evidence. The phrase "the admissibility or inadmissibility of evidence" includes the qualification or disqualification of a person to be a witness and the existence or nonexistence of a privilege.
PREPONDERANCE - Outweighing.
PRESENTMENT - A report by a grand jury on something they have investigated on their own knowledge.
PRESUMPTION - An assumption of fact resulting from a rule of law which requires such fact to be assumed from another fact or group of facts found or otherwise established in the action.
PRIMA FACUE - At first sight.
PRIMA FACIE CASE - A case where the evidence is very patent against the defendant.
PRINCIPAL - The source of authority or rights; a person primarily liable as differentiated from "principle" as a primary or basic doctrine.
PRO AND CON - For and against.
PRO RATA - Proportionally.
PROBATE - Relating to proof, especially to the proof of wills.
PROBATIVE - Tending to prove.
PROCEDURE - In law, this term generally denotes rules which are established by the Federal, State, or local Governments regarding the types of pleading and courtroom practice which must be followed by the parties involved in a criminal or civil case.
PROCLAMATION - A public notice by an official of some order, intended action, or state of facts.

PROFFERED EVIDENCE - The admissibility or inadmissibility of which is dependent upon the existence or nonexistence of a preliminary fact.
PROMISSORY (NOTE) - A promise in writing to pay a specified sum at an expressed time, or on demand, or at sight, to a named person, or to his order, or bearer.
PROOF - The establishment by evidence of a requisite degree of belief concerning a fact in the mind of the trier of fact or the court.
PROPERTY - Includes both real and personal property.
PROPRIETARY (adj.) - Relating or pertaining to ownership; usually a single owner.
PROSECUTE - To carry on an action or other judicial proceeding; to proceed against a person criminally.
PROVISO - A limitation or condition in a legal instrument.
PROXIMATE - Immediate; nearest
PUBLIC EMPLOYEE - An officer, agent, or employee of a public entity.
PUBLIC ENTITY - Includes a national, state, county, city and county, city, district, public authority, public agency, or any other political subdivision or public corporation, whether foreign or domestic.
PUBLIC OFFICIAL - Includes an official of a political dubdivision of such state or territory and of a municipality.
PUNITIVE - Relating to punishment.

Q

QUASH - To make void.
QUASI - As if; as it were.
QUID PRO QUO - Something for something; the giving of one valuable thing for another.
QUITCLAIM (v.) - To release or relinquish claim or title to, especially in deeds to realty.
QUO WARRANTO - A legal procedure to test an official's right to a public office or the right to hold a franchise, or to hold an office in a domestic corporation.

R

RATIFY - To approve and sanction.
REAL PROPERTY - Includes lands, tenements, and hereditaments.
REALTY - A brief term for real property.
REBUT - To contradict; to refute, especially by evidence and arguments.
RECEIVER - A person who is appointed by the court to receive, and hold in trust property in litigation.
RECIDIVIST - Habitual criminal.
RECIPROCAL - Mutual.
RECOUPMENT - To keep back or get something which is due; also, it is the right of a defendant to have a deduction from the amount of the plaintiff's damages because the plaintiff has not fulfilled his part of the same contract.
RECROSS EXAMINATION - Examination of a witness by a cross-examiner subsequent to a redirect examination of the witness.
REDEEM - To release an estate or article from mortgage or pledge by paying the debt for which it stood as security.
REDIRECT EXAMINATION - Examination of a witness by the direct examiner subsequent to the cross-examination of the witness.
REFEREE - A person to whom a cause pending in a court is referred by the court, to take testimony, hear the parties, and report thereon to the court.

REFERENDUM - A method of submitting an important legislative or administrative matter to a direct vote of the people.
RELEVANT EVIDENCE - Evidence including evidence relevant to the credulity of a witness or hearsay declarant, having any tendency in reason to prove or disprove any disputed fact that is of consequence to the determination of the action.
REMAND - To send a case back to the lower court from which it came, for further proceedings.
REPLEVIN - An action to recover goods or chattels wrongfully taken or detained.
REPLY (REPLICATION) - Generally, a reply is what the plaintiff or other person who has instituted proceedings says in answer to the defendant's case.
RE JUDICATA - A thing judicially acted upon or decided.
RES ADJUDICATA - Doctrine that an issue or dispute litigated and determined in a case between the opposing parties is deemed permanently decided between these parties.
RESCIND (RECISSION) - To avoid or cancel a contract.
RESPONDENT - A defendant in a proceeding in chancery or admiralty; also, the person who contends against the appeal in a case.
RESTITUTION - In equity, it is the restoration of both parties to their original condition (when practicable), upon the rescission of a contract for fraud or similar cause.
RETROACTIVE (RETROSPECTIVE) - Looking back; effective as of a prior time.
REVERSED - A term used by appellate courts to indicate that the decision of the lower court in the case before it has been set aside.
REVOKE - To recall or cancel.
RIPARIAN (RIGHTS) - The rights of a person owning land containing or bordering on a water course or other body of water, such as lakes and rivers.

S

SALE - A contract whereby the ownership of property is transferred from one person to another for a sum of money or for any consideration.
SANCTION - A penalty or punishment provided as a means of enforcing obedience to a law; also, an authorization.
SATISFACTION - The discharge of an obligation by paying a party what is due to him; or what is awarded to him by the judgment of a court or otherwise.
SCIENTER - Knowingly; also, it is used in pleading to denote the defendant's guilty knowledge.
SCINTILLA - A spark; also the least particle.
SECRET OF STATE - Governmental secret relating to the national defense or the international relations of the United States.
SECURITY - Indemnification; the term is applied to an obligation, such as a mortgage or deed of trust, given by a debtor to insure the payment or performance of his debt, by furnishing the creditor with a resource to be used in case of the debtor's failure to fulfill the principal obligation.
SENTENCE - The judgment formally pronounced by the court or judge upon the defendant after his conviction in a criminal prosecution.
SET-OFF - A claim or demand which one party in an action credits against the claim of the opposing party.
SHALL and MAY - "Shall" is mandatory and "may" is permissive.
SITUS - Location.
SOVEREIGN - A person, body or state in which independent and supreme authority is vested.
STARE DECISIS - To follow decided cases.

STATE - "State" means this State, unless applied to the different parts of the United States. In the latter case, it includes any state, district, commonwealth, territory or insular possession of the United States, including the District of Columbia.
STATEMENT - (a) Oral or written verbal expression or (b) nonverbal conduct of a person intended by him as a substitute for oral or written verbal expression.
STATUTE - An act of the legislature. Includes a treaty.
STATUTE OF LIMITATION - A statute limiting the time to bring an action after the right of action has arisen.
STAY - To hold in abeyance an order of a court.
STIPULATION - Any agreement made by opposing attorneys regulating any matter incidental to the proceedings or trial.
SUBORDINATION (AGREEMENT) - An agreement making one's rights inferior to or of a lower rank than another's.
SUBORNATION - The crime of procuring a person to lie or to make false statements to a court.
SUBPOENA - A writ or order directed to a person, and requiring his attendance at a particular time and place to testify as a witness.
SUBPOENA DUCES TECUM - A subpoena used, not only for the purpose of compelling witnesses to attend in court, but also requiring them to bring with them books or documents which may be in their possession, and which may tend to elucidate the subject matter of the trial.
SUBROGATION - The substituting of one for another as a creditor, the new creditor succeeding to the former's rights.
SUBSIDY - A government grant to assist a private enterprise deemed advantageous to the public.
SUI GENERIS - Of the same kind.
SUIT - Any civil proceeding by a person or persons against another or others in a court of justice by which the plaintiff pursues the remedies afforded him by law.
SUMMONS - A notice to a defendant that an action against him has been commenced and requiring him to appear in court and answer the complaint.
SUPRA - Above; this word occurring by itself in a book refers the reader to a previous part of the book.
SURETY - A person who binds himself for the payment of a sum of money, or for the performance of something else, for another.
SURPLUSAGE - Extraneous or unnecessary matter.
SURVIVORSHIP - A term used when a person becomes entitled to property by reason of his having survived another person who had an interest in the property.
SUSPEND SENTENCE - Hold back a sentence pending good behavior of prisoner.
SYLLABUS - A note prefixed to a report, especially a case, giving a brief statement of the court's ruling on different issues of the case.

T

TALESMAN - Person summoned to fill a panel of jurors.
TENANT - One who holds or possesses lands by any kind of right or title; also, one who has the temporary use and occupation of real property owned by another person (landlord), the duration and terms of his tenancy being usually fixed by an instrument called "a lease."
TENDER - An offer of money; an expression of willingness to perform a contract according to its terms.
TERM - When used with reference to a court, it signifies the period of time during which the court holds a session, usually of several weeks or months duration.

TESTAMENTARY - Pertaining to a will or the administration of a will.
TESTATOR (male)
TESTATRIX (female) - One who makes or has made a testament or will.
TESTIFY (TESTIMONY) - To give evidence under oath as a witness.
TO WIT - That is to say; namely.
TORT - Wrong; injury to the person.
TRANSITORY - Passing from place to place.
TRESPASS - Entry into another's ground, illegally.
TRIAL - The examination of a cause, civil or criminal, before a judge who has jurisdiction over it, according to the laws of the land.
TRIER OF FACT - Includes (a) the jury and (b) the court when the court is trying an issue of fact other than one relating to the admissibility of evidence.
TRUST - A right of property, real or personal, held by one party for the benefit of another.
TRUSTEE - One who lawfully holds property in custody for the benefit of another.

U

UNAVAILABLE AS A WITNESS - The declarant is (1) Exempted or precluded on the ground of privilege from testifying concerning the matter to which his statement is relevant; (2) Disqualified from testifying to the matter; (3) Dead or unable to attend or to testify at the hearing because of then existing physical or mental illness or infirmity; (4) Absent from the hearing and the court is unable to compel his attendance by its process; or (5) Absent from the hearing and the proponent of his statement has exercised reasonable diligence but has been unable to procure his attendance by the court's process.
ULTRA VIRES - Acts beyond the scope and power of a corporation, association, etc.
UNILATERAL - One-sided; obligation upon, or act of one party.
USURY - Unlawful interest on a loan.

V

VACATE - To set aside; to move out.
VARIANCE - A discrepancy or disagreement between two instruments or two aspects of the same case, which by law should be consistent.
VENDEE - A purchaser or buyer.
VENDOR - The person who transfers property by sale, particularly real estate; the term "seller" is used more commonly for one who sells personal property.
VENIREMEN - Persons ordered to appear to serve on a jury or composing a panel of jurors.
VENUE - The place at which an action is tried, generally based on locality or judicial district in which an injury occurred or a material fact happened.
VERDICT - The formal decision or finding of a jury.
VERIFY - To confirm or substantiate by oath.
VEST - To accrue to.
VOID - Having no legal force or binding effect.
VOIR DIRE - Preliminary examination of a witness or a juror to test competence, interest, prejudice, etc.

W

WAIVE - To give up a right.
WAIVER - The intentional or voluntary relinquishment of a known right.
WARRANT (WARRANTY) (v.) - To promise that a certain fact or state of facts, in relation to the subject matter, is, or shall be, as it is represented to be.

WARRANT (n.) - A writ issued by a judge, or other competent authority, addressed to a sheriff, or other officer, requiring him to arrest the person therein named, and bring him before the judge or court to answer or be examined regarding the offense with which he is charged.

WRIT - An order or process issued in the name of the sovereign or in the name of a court or judicial officer, commanding the performance or nonperformance of some act.

WRITING - Handwriting, typewriting, printing, photostating, photographing and every other means of recording upon any tangible thing any form of communication or representation, including letters, words, pictures, sounds, or symbols, or combinations thereof.

WRITINGS AND RECORDINGS - Consists of letters, words, or numbers, or their equivalent, set down by handwriting, typewriting, printing, photostating, photographing, magnetic impulse, mechanical or electronic recording, or other form of data compilation.

Y

YEA AND NAY - Yes and no.

YELLOW DOG CONTRACT - A contract by which employer requires employee to sign an instrument promising as condition that he will not join a union during its continuance, and will be discharged if he does join.

Z

ZONING - The division of a city by legislative regulation into districts and the prescription and application in each district of regulations having to do with structural and architectural designs of buildings and of regulations prescribing use to which buildings within designated districts may be put.

CPSIA information can be obtained
at www.ICGtesting.com
Printed in the USA
BVHW071342231219
567575BV00014B/441